THE WALLS OF ISRAEL

THE WALLS
OF ISRAEL

by Jean Lartéguy

Translated by Ormonde de Kay, Jr.

Foreword by Moshe Dayan

M Evans
Lanham • New York • Boulder • Toronto • Plymouth, UK

M. Evans
An imprint of The Rowman & Littlefield Publishing Group, Inc.
4501 Forbes Boulevard, Suite 200, Lanham, Maryland 20706
http://www.rlpgtrade.com

10 Thornbury Road, Plymouth PL6 7PP, United Kingdom

Distributed by National Book Network

British Library Cataloguing in Publication Information Available

Library of Congress Cataloging-in-Publication Data Available

ISBN 13: 978-1-59077-366-6 (pbk: alk. paper)

♾™ The paper used in this publication meets the minimum requirements of American National Standard for Information Sciences—Permanence of Paper for Printed Library Materials, ANSI/NISO Z39.48-1992.

Printed in the United States of America

Foreword

To explain the victory of the Tsahal (the army of Israel) in the Six-Day War, it is not enough to talk about our character and our soldiers' sacrifices. These are, to be sure, important factors, but they don't explain everything.

During these last ten years I have not been in direct and continuous contact with the army. It was only on the eve of the war that I came to realize the progress it had made. It had learned how to adapt its armored units as well as its paratroopers and air force to the peculiar requirements of this unique area of the Middle East where it is destined to fight. This experience, acquired over ten years, helps to explain the "lightning victory." But that is still not the whole story.

As long as Israel has existed, in time of peace as in time of war, it has been surrounded by enemies who think only of destroying it.

Yet never, since 1948, has Israel protected its frontiers with a network of barbed wire or a line of fortifications. To the chiefs of the Israeli army, the best defense has always been, and remains today, offense—attacking the enemy on his own territory.

To understand this, it was enough to visit Golan Heights after they were taken. The Syrians there had literally buried themselves in deep bunkers; they lived in concrete shelters surrounded by barbed wire to a width of several hundred yards. In addition, on the Golan Heights overlooking the Huleh Valley the Syrians were in a very strong position. They knew that Israel had no intention of invading Syria, but all the same they barricaded themselves on those heights.

Below, in the valleys, are Israeli villages. In each one a shelter had been dug and some barbed wire strung around it. But the valley was open to the fire from enemy tanks, which held the heights and could pound up the whole area under cultivation with their shells.

In case of war, those flimsy shelters and three rolls of barbed wire would not have saved the inhabitants of the valley; they knew from the start that their only hope was to hurl themselves forward in the teeth of the enemy.

The Syrians, on the other hand, were dug in on their heights and conceived of the war as exclusively defensive. They did not want to come out of their bunkers.

Our strength, that of our officers and soldiers, arose from this principle: We shall never take shelter behind barbed wire or man-made fortifications; we shall charge the enemy and hurl him back onto his own territory. This principle Nasser has never grasped.

Then, too, there is the younger generation. The army chiefs during this "lightning war" were the same young people we had been accustomed to call the "caffé espresso generation," in contrast to the generation that had fought the war of independence in 1948. In 1948 we were, to be sure, more idealistic and less concerned with pursuing individual careers. But the Israeli soldiers, like their officers, have never forgotten that they must continue to meet exacting standards of ability and training that force them to live the same life of absolute idealism that the "old ones" knew. This is so true that a gulf has opened up today between the values current in civilian life and those in military life.

Within the army there is still no class distinction whatever. All the young officers are trained in the same military schools, according to the same rules. The officers have learned never to fight behind their men but as much as possible in front of them. Thus, of the fifty men lost by the Golani brigade on the Syrian plateau, thirty-five were officers. This was no accident.

That is the secret of our army's strength. It remains as incomprehensible to the Egyptians as it did to their Soviet instructors. We went to war to open up the Strait of Tiran, but when Jordan joined the Egyptians we conquered western Jordan as far as the Jordan River and liberated Jerusalem. Then Syria came into the war, and we conquered the Golan Heights. No one, neither myself nor anyone else, had foreseen that things would end this way. In six days, our army, fighting on all the borders of Israel, mapped out the frontiers on which we now stand.

General Moshe Dayan, Minister of Defense, Israel

Contents

Prologue:
Ambuscade on the Jordan

I am getting ready to go out on ambush with a small unit of Israeli paratroopers. We are going to station ourselves a few yards from the Jordan River at a crossing point for the commandos of al-Fatah. There the river, a dark-green corridor through the blazing desert, widens to form a ford where men and flocks can cross. It was at this point that the Essene St. John the Baptist reputedly baptised Jesus by immersion and initiated him into the secrets of the sect from which Christianity was to develop.

Behind us to the north is Jericho, with its flame trees in bloom, its hot streets pulsing with life. Nasal strains drift out of the cafés, where Arabs smoke their water pipes as if nothing had ever happened there. Farther south is the Allenby Bridge, or what is left of it: a pile of twisted scrap iron.

Another bridge, built jointly by Israelis and Jordanians, has replaced it. But cooperation between the two countries has never been more remote. One morning, on this bridge, a Jordanian soldier murdered an Israeli soldier who had come to talk with him, as had been his habit.

The Israelis continue to occupy all of Jordan west of the river, the richest part of King Hussein's former domain. Today most of the bases are located in what is left of Jordanian territory. By day, cars and trucks constantly pass back and forth between Jordan and "Greater Israel." A veritable flood of commerce is maintained between Amman and the territories that the Arabs lost in the war. But at 5:00 P.M. traffic stops, and when night falls the war is resumed again until morning.

Still farther south is the Dead Sea, that pit of brackish water in a petrified landscape. Here we are assembled, more than 800 feet below sea level. The heat is almost unbearable. It is 7:00 P.M. The sergeant assembles his men. He explains firmly the route we shall take, the tactics that will be employed, and the passwords and signals in case of an encounter. The Israeli soldier always likes to know the why and how of his orders, which is perhaps one reason why he is capable of taking the place of his officer or adjutant at any moment in combat.

The sergeant's words are being translated for me, but I am listening with only one ear. I cannot take my eyes off three small wooden crosses stuck in the ground a few yards away. Two days ago, three men of al-Fatah were killed and buried there. I ask my interpreter, a young pied noir from North Africa, "Why the crosses? They were Moslems."

He replies, astonished, "But sir, in westerns, when they bury some guy they've gunned down, they always put up a cross."

Like all his buddies, he lives half in the war and half in cowboy movies. In only a few years he has become a true Israeli, a soldier who kills in cold blood if he must, without hatred, who does not loot, does not rape, does not burn, and does not boast.

For a moment I picture the life he could have had in Tunis, where the Arab and Western worlds meet and the citizens believe in neither one nor the other. At twenty he would already be disillusioned, beginning to grow fat in the back of a shop. He would be bored and he would be making money. At twenty-five he would be old. But he has been recast in the crucible that is the Israeli army. It has given him another body, lean and tanned, with supple muscles. It has taught him to sleep very little or not at all and to speak another language: Hebrew, which was dead and has been brought to life again. It has also given him a country to defend and some very simple reasons for fighting and dying.

He resumes translating the sergeant's "lecture" for me.

"It's all very simple," the sergeant is saying. "When we get to the ambush we form a semicircle, with each man touching the man to his left and his right. That way, if anybody falls asleep, his neighbor will feel it. Remember your buddies who have had their throats cut like sheep because they dozed off.

"Your weapons will be in front of you, loaded and with the safety catch off, ready to fire. Don't stir until the al-Fatah men are within five yards. When I give the command—and not until then—grab your submachine gun, and, from a prone position, fire your first volley.

"Then, all together, we stand up and fire the rest of the round. While we are reloading, the machine gun will fire one full round, to cover us. Then, still in formation so as not to fire on one another, we withdraw, finishing off the wounded and killing those we missed.

"I remind you that during the entire ambuscade nobody talks, nobody smokes, nobody moves, and nobody goes to sleep.

"Don't forget to put on the mosquito repellant; otherwise you'll be eaten alive."

THE DEPARTURE

I must submit to a certain number of rituals before I can accompany the paratroopers on their ambuscade. First, they read aloud to me in the presence of witnesses the text of an oath which I must then sign in I don't know how many copies. I pledge myself, my ancestors, and my descendants never to claim so much as a single Israeli pound (40 cents) from the state of Israel if I am killed or wounded. I also pledge myself not to reveal all sorts of things that have only the most tenuous connection with what I am going to see. I have taken many such oaths for armies that I have followed to action, but never has the whole thing been treated with such importance and ceremony. At first I thought they were pulling my leg. Now I know otherwise, that the matter is both simpler and more complex: In Israel everything that has to do with the army is sacred.

Next I must put on a uniform, those same olive drab fatigues that are becoming the uniform of all the world's armies. The Israelis themselves wear fatigues or camouflaged uniforms. They are clean-shaven or have moustaches, and their hair can be long or cut short. I listen to a little discussion verging on dandyism between two paratroopers. One turns to me: "Look at my jacket; it's a French paratrooper's uniform. They're the best and the best cut. They're in great demand. A whole stock of them was sent to us when they were confiscated from some of our paratroopers who were being disciplined!"

Someone hands me a weapon, an Uzi submachine gun, small and quick-firing but somewhat heavy for its size. The Israeli soldiers prefer the Soviet Kalachnikov assault gun. I also receive two ammunition clips.

I share a quick meal with the soldiers: raw fruit and vegetables, fried eggs, and pot cheese. The food is the same everywhere, whether in the kibbutzim or in the army—healthy but without much variety. The meat is always tasteless. By Hebrew religious law slaughtered cattle must, in effect, be completely drained of blood. We swallow a cup of bad coffee, smoke a last cigarette, and move out by a path leading up to a ridge. Night has fallen, without bringing the slightest breath of air. Laboriously we struggle ahead in a real sweatbox.

Up ahead are the sergeant and a scout. In the Israeli army the commander always goes first, whether he is a sergeant, a captain, a colonel, or even a general. Hence the staggering proportion of officers killed during the Six-Day War—30 percent.

The Jordan is about half a mile away. But, to reach the ford where the al-Fatah men cross without being seen by them, we walk for more than an hour, circling around and doubling back in order to take advantage of every little bit of cover. One must be careful not to stumble on this arid terrain, which crunches underfoot in some places and is packed hard in others.

The sergeant signals us to stop. He goes on ahead with the scout, bayonet in hand, to find out whether or not the position has been mined.

Palestinian commandos and Israeli paratroopers are involved in deadly guerilla warfare. Just as the paratroopers know all the crossing points of al-Fatah, al-Fatah men themselves know all the places where the paratroopers can set ambuscades, and sometimes they mine them before the Israelis get there.

We are now lying on our stomachs, motionless. I need only put out a hand to touch my submachine gun. I wonder what I would do if al-Fatah commandos were suddenly to loom up before me. This war is not mine, and this land is not promised to me, for I am not Jewish.

The sergeant, stretched out next to me, touches my elbow and whispers, "There'll be some game tonight."

The "game" is young Palestinians, educated for the most part in the universities of West Europe or Lebanon. They are summarily trained in camps around Amman by Russian or Algerian instructors and then sent across the frontier in groups of seven or eight to plant mines along the roads and to attack, with bazookas, the new Israeli military colonies established in the conquered territories. They are brave, still inexperienced, but always very well armed. All those who are captured or killed are found to be equipped with the most up-to-date Soviet matériel: the famous Kalachnikov assault gun that all paratroopers dream of possessing, grenades, explosives, delayed-action mines, and walkie-talkies.

Gone are the days of those Palestinian resistance organizations, mainstays of Egyptian propaganda, that served mainly to enrich their leaders, pot-bellied and moustachioed carnival roustabouts armed to the teeth. They never ceased to boast of their imaginary feats of arms: If a train was derailed they took the credit, if a plane crashed they claimed the score, and if a wall fell on Moshe Dayan's head while he was digging at an archeological site (with that astonishing imprudence that characterizes him) they, as usual, were behind it. In reality, however, they hardly ever left their camps except to fire a few moonlight rounds at the kibbutzim on the other side of the frontier. When the war broke out these chiefs fled, and in the Gaza Strip the lean Israeli warriors used grenades to clean out the nests where a few of these gross parasites still huddled. In their caches were found provisions, sums of money, and an incredible arsenal.

The new generation of al-Fatah men did not make its appearance until a year later. (By the term "al-Fatah men" I mean members of all the various Palestinian resistance organizations: the Popular Front for the Liberation of Palestine; the Palestinian commandos reconstituted from the liberation organizations that Nasser formerly protected; and al-Fatah itself, with its military arm al-Assifah.)

These new resistance fighters are neither grotesque nor ridiculous. They are in the pay of neither a "socialist" head of state, an oil monarch, nor any secret service whatever. They are no longer burdened with an ideology; they simply want to reconquer their lost land. The very young soldiers of the Israeli army are even beginning to feel a certain respect for them.

Yes, what would I do if young Palestinians suddenly loomed up in front of me? I push the question from my mind, hoping that I won't be confronted with this problem that I don't know how to resolve.

Without making a sound, I roll over on my back. Overhead stretches the whole sky of Palestine, glittering with stars, a sky as dark and as soft as velvet.

These same stars guided the biblical shepherds and the soldiers of Joshua who crossed the Jordan at this very spot and took advantage of an earthquake to capture Jericho a few kilometers away. Then came the Roman legions, the horsemen of Allach, Crusaders encased in steel, and Egyptian Mamelukes in the service of the Turks. They passed on, each group leaving its imprint on this land too heavily burdened with history, with holy places, with tombs of prophets and patriarchs. Today, 2.2 million twentieth-century Jews from all the countries of the world, thanks to their character and their technology, hold in check 70 million Arabs scarcely out of the Middle Ages. For the Arabs are still fundamentally living in the Middle Ages, even though they boast so-called "socialist" governments and even though they are equipped with such ultramodern weapons as nuclear warheads and infrared guns, which they don't know how to use.

THE YOUNG MEN OF MAY

An ambuscade is a lengthy affair. I forget the young volunteers of al-Fatah in thinking about those students who at this very moment are fighting the C.R.S. [Compagnies républicaines de sécurité, or state security police] in the streets of Paris.

Before leaving the camp, I listened to the news from France on a transistor. It was fragmentary: Students were throwing up barricades and occupying the Latin Quarter; 400 people had been wounded; the trade unions were calling for a strike; de Gaulle's courtiers had even dared to get him out of bed.

The Israeli paratroopers are all between eighteen and twenty-one years old, the age of the students on the barricades; they have been very kind, even considerate, as if I am the one who is sick. Alas, it is my country that is sick, from old age, from fear of its young people, from being governed by an irascible, imperious, anachronistic old man who long ago formed a particular idea of the world and its people and clings to it still.

But Israel has fashioned, from among one of the oldest peoples in the world, from descendants of those who survived ghettos and concentration camps, the youngest army in the world.

Rocket flares light up the night at regular intervals of a few minutes. The big guns boom in front of us. Are they in Syria or in Jordan? I can no longer tell, with all these interlocking frontiers.

The sergeant touches me on the elbow again and passes a canteen of coffee. For two months he has been with his unit on the banks of the Jordan, two months during which, on every second night, from 8:00 in the evening until 5:00 in the morning, he has lain with his men in the parched riverbed or, as now, simply stretched out on the ground, waiting for the Palestinian commandos to come.

At twenty years he is a veteran of the Six-Day War; he fought in the Sinai Desert and on the Golan Heights of Syria; he has killed and risked being killed. He will spend three of the best years of his life under arms. When he goes home he will remain a reserve soldier for twenty years. My sergeant does not concern himself with, and is not in the least anxious about, either the future of Marxism or the future of the consumer society; he thinks only about the future of his country, the survival or destruction of Israel. He cannot understand what is going on in France or the frustrated hunger for adventure that haunts so many sons of the middle-class and makes revolutionaries of them. If he wants to live the collectivist life (of an absolute collectivism such as has never been attempted in the U.S.S.R. or even in China) he can enter a kibbutz. He can also try—in Tel Aviv, Beersheba, Haifa, or elsewhere—to carve out a place for himself in a consumer society only slightly less developed than our own.

But that is not his problem. He knows that he will have to fight for a good part of his life if his country is to survive, that he belongs to an army that does not have the right to lose a single battle, and that this will be so for a very long time to come. For him, all the rest is so much idle talk.

But he is not at all a robot soldier, a heel-clicking machine that says yes and kills. He is, in fact, the very opposite: an intelligent young man, profoundly individualistic, who does not like to hear a lot of bull. Throughout my observation of the Israeli army I was "endowed" with a lieutenant from the security services. He was officially charged with arranging appointments and passes for me, but his real task was to keep watch on me and to prevent me from discovering the famous army secrets which, as we shall see, do not exist. He was at once the best-intentioned and clumsiest of propagandists. His name was Hilan. Hilan had one amusing run-in with the sergeant. As he was extolling to me the healthy, active, dedicated life of these boys who would rather guard the frontiers than be back in training, wasting their time eating ice cream and chasing girls in town, the sergeant asked him in excellent French who he thought he was kidding. The lieutenant chewed him out in Hebrew, but the sergeant simply shrugged his shoulders.

I know what Hilan said to him: that it is in Israel's interest to stuff my head with propaganda and that, in any case, as I am neither a Jew nor an Israeli, they have no leverage on me and need to be careful. But the sergeant thought me a "good head"; he had read all my books and liked them. He found it rather amusing that an old man like myself was going along with them on an ambuscade, whereas Hilan, who was their age and had just discovered that he had a cold, had sacked out under his mosquito netting. (At my age, forty-seven, one is an old man in the Israeli army; the age limit for an army chief of staff, that is, the commander in chief, is forty-five. General Yitzhak Rabin, who had reached that limit, left the army immediately after the Six-Day War to become Israel's ambassador in Washington, D.C.)

The machine gunner is falling asleep. I feel it in the slackening of his whole body next to mine. The sergeant wakes him with a kick and curses him in a low voice. Only a little while ago they were horsing around together like kids; they were at ease and equals. But not now.

What a strange army this is, both disciplined and undisciplined, badly equipped and so well trained. The soldiers are always ready to debate their orders, but to the last man they will risk their lives to carry them out.

In a film on the Six-Day War produced by the army, which I saw in a theatre in Tel Aviv, I was struck by this comment: "The whole army was waiting for the order to fight. There were 150,000 chiefs of staff tirelessly discussing measures necessary to win this war."

The chauffeur speaks familiarly to the general he drives and calls him by his first name. The general's pay at its highest is hardly more than the wages of a skilled worker in France. The Israeli army has no unified philosophy; it deals from day to day with problems as they arise. It follows the theories of no one school of war, French, English, or American. It is neither for Clausewitz nor for Guderian; it borrows whatever seems useful from any source. It wins all its wars—because it cannot afford to lose a single one—with obsolete equipment twenty years older than that of its enemy, which goes to show that man, even in war, is still superior to the machine.

At the same table colonels and simple soldiers all eat the same food, which is "kosher"—that is, prepared according to biblical principles but not to those of gastronomy—even though 80 percent of the soldiers in this modern army are atheists or even frankly antireligious.

The soldier neither salutes nor stands at attention, but he is dedicated to the childish cult of secrecy. He sees spies everywhere and is encouraged to see them. Still burdened with influences from the Diaspora and the ghettos, he considers the slightest criticism of his country proof of anti-Semitism.

I have never ceased to be astonished by the Israelis. I vacillate from admiration to exasperation and back again several times a day. Israel is at one and the same time Sparta and Athens, discipline and disorder, perpetual argument and absolute obedience to orders, asceticism and horseplay, pride and anxiety, faith and doubt. And always there is that stabbing question which everyone, corporals as well as the highest generals, puts to me: "What do you think of us? Aren't we in the right? Isn't our cause just?"

They want approval and admiration without reservation. And on many counts they have earned approval and admiration. Without question they are the best and bravest soldiers in the whole Middle East, for they have faith in that miracle of which they are the guardians.

In *Promise and Fulfilment,* Arthur Koestler writes:

Imprisoned in a petrified faith, the Jews have for many centuries lived on familiar terms with the supernatural and quite out of touch with nature. Hence the naïveté of their enchantment at seeing Jewish cows, Jewish grass, Jewish tomatoes and Jewish eggs. They marvel at the chick, which, scarcely out of the egg, already knows how to peck for food; to them, it seems every bit as admirable as the child prodigies who at the age of seven know by heart entire chapters of holy scripture. The green plains of Israel were born of a double desert: of the land without water and of the arid past of the nation.

But the Jews of Israel marvel still more at having their own army, with tanks and planes, with corporals and generals—

an army that knows how to fight, that is essentially prepared for one kind of war and fights it better than anyone else. This army is the shield of David and the ramparts of Israel, the crucible in which a nation has been forged from disparate elements. In an important sense, the army *is* Israel, for without it the nation would have long since ceased to exist. Sand would have again settled over Tel Aviv and the kibbutzim of the Negev. The desert that is everywhere in retreat would have reclaimed its ancient domain. The soldiers of Nasser and the Bedouin of the Arab Legion would have amused themselves with little Jewish girls before slaughtering them. Then they would have set fire to the forests and the factories. The few thousand survivors of the promised land that had been redeemed would again have known the Diaspora, the despair of becoming wandering Jews once more.

Suddenly, the two bodies alongside me stiffen. There is a sound in front of us, a sound that is difficult to identify: the rustling of a reed, a foot stumbling on a root. Hands reach for weapons. Then the sound stops. Another flare bathes the countryside in its harsh light. It dangles for a few moments from its parachute and then goes out. A false alarm. The bodies relax.

It must have been an animal, some fox or badger out hunting or returning to its lair. There are a great many wild animals in Israel because no one hunts them. Game killed by a gun is not "kosher"—that is, it is impure because it has not been slaughtered in accordance with the sacred rituals of the Bible—and therefore cannot be eaten. In Galilee and on the Golan Heights of Syria I have seen countless flocks of partridges so fat that they could barely lift themselves out of the path of my car.

Silence again; but like all silences, this one is peopled with sounds: A paratrooper whispers; another stirs a fraction of an inch because he has a cramp. This is certainly the first time I have witnessed an ambuscade of this kind. No attempt is made to take shelter; on the contrary, the men lie flat on the ground, waiting for the moment to leap to their feet.

Here I see again the entire tactic of the Israeli army. It is the same at the lowest echelon, a combat group commanded by a sergeant, as at the highest, a tank brigade led by a colonel or general in a rush upon an enemy dug in behind fortifications with weapons more modern and far more powerful than his. It can be summed up in a single word: audacity. It means seeking hand-to-hand combat at any price; it means refusal to take shelter and protection. But this tactic, like everything in Israel, is actually very carefully worked out behind its mask of improvisation. It is tailored to the enemy, to his fear of close combat, to his too-vivid imagination, which shows him a night full of thousands of enemies, when there is only a handful.

This is indeed a strange army, at one with the whole nation!

THE TWENTIETH ANNIVERSARY

On the ambuscade I cannot even talk to all those boys whose bodies touch mine. I cannot even ask them what they think, what they want, how they see their future and their country's future, whether they have accustomed themselves to the idea that for years to come war will be their only real occupation. One of them, the machine gunner, told me earlier:

"I am from Jerusalem. The first time I went back there on leave after the reunification I just couldn't stop walking around. At last I could go through the Mandelbaum Gate without being fired upon, to the Wailing Wall to see the Hasidim jig up and down in their robes and curls. You know,

I prefer the Old City, the suqs of the Arab quarter, the shish
kebab, the Arab tea and coffee."

I cannot resist: I touch his shoulder, he turns toward me,
and I ask him (in Spanish because he was born in the distant
Americas), "Why are you here?" He whistles softly between
his teeth the opening bars of the song, "Jerusalem the
Golden," and I remember the strange nocturnal parade that
I witnessed on April 30, 1968. It was three days before the
great military parade marking the twentieth anniversary of
the creation of Israel. Such, at least, was the official reason
for the celebration; in reality, it was to be the solemn nuptial
rite uniting Jerusalem and the army—a marriage until death.

The Tsahal, the army, was practicing for the event; practice was needed, for the Tsahal is no parade army. Also the
commanders don't much like to use equipment and waste
gasoline on these vain expressions of military pride. Much too
pragmatic for that, they rest their pride on a higher plane.
But this time the army had to parade, because the Security
Council had forbidden it to, because it was necessary to take
up the challenge, and above all because Israel had to set its
seal for all time on the long-awaited reunification of Jerusalem.

Only the journalists had been alerted to this rehearsal,
which took place between 2:00 and 4:00 in the morning
under the walls of the Old City. Naïvely, I had thought we
would be a mere handful. But 50,000 people, mysteriously
forewarned, were massed along the route, watching their
soldiers pass and repass in the glow from the trucks' headlights. This crowd did not applaud and did not speak. It could
see only shadowy figures dragging their feet to show their
disgust, yet the crowd did not tire of contemplating its
miracle: The victorious soldiers whom the world admires
were its sons.

On the day before the parade Israelis came by the hundreds of thousands from the farthest corners of Israel: the

kibbutzniks of Galilee and the Negev with their crownless cloth caps; the fishermen from the Lake of Tiberias; the *moshavniks* of Be'er Tuvya, who raise Danish cattle; sunburned workers from the potash works of Sodom; *pieds noirs* from Morocco, Algeria, and Tunisia settled at Beersheba, the gateway to the desert, who talk with the accents of Bab al-Oued, Bône and Tunis. There were girls and boys carrying guns or military caps or, having neither, walking with their arms around each others' necks or hand in hand; there were boy scouts and soldiers. They surged around the city walls, blocking all traffic. They sang, they shouted, they danced, and they pounded with thousands of little plastic hammers that made an unbearable noise when they struck: *tsweet! tsweet!* When night fell thousands of fires sprang up in the valleys and on the heights surrounding or overlooking Jerusalem. Men and women roasted meat; they danced and sang all through the night and didn't go to bed until morning. The night was cool, for we were half a mile above sea level, but also very clear, of a blue that was hardly dark at all.

I found myself on the hill of Neve Sah'anan, below the national museum, with the guests of Teddy Kollek, Mayor of Jerusalem. He is a stocky man who wears his collar open and his shirt outside his trousers: the dress uniform of the kibbutzniks. Up there behind the ramparts, there were still 70,000 Christian and Moslem Arabs who had refused to accept the conquest and had locked themselves in behind the lowered curtains of their shops. They compared the Jews of Israel to the Crusaders, who had stayed for a century and then departed. "These too will leave, like the knights of St. Louis and Godefroy de Bouillon, but sooner, for history has speeded up. All we have to do is wait."

But the army and the people of Israel have decided that they will never again leave Jerusalem, even if it means being exterminated to the last man, woman, and child.

How beautiful was the bride, Jerusalem the Golden, with its walls illuminated by floodlights! It was the city of David and Solomon, of the Temple and the Wailing Wall, but it was also the city of the tomb of Christ and the mosque of Omar. Jerusalem was not the holy city of the Jews alone.

Teddy Kollek, solidly planted on his feet and with his hands in his pockets, gazed out over the city while his guests, stretched out on mats before a big fire, passed meat, cakes, and bottles of Israeli cognac and soft drinks. A woman with a deep voice intoned the theme song of the Six-Day War:

If I forget thee, Jerusalem, Jerusalem of pure gold,
May thy name burn my lips, like the kiss of the angel of fire.
Jerusalem of gold, of copper, and of light. . . .

The Arabs, during the period when everyone had been waiting for the war to begin, had had another hymn, coarse and indefensible, to which Oum Kalsoum had lent her admirable voice. It went: "Slaughter. . . . slaughter." If only for that, they deserved to be defeated.

I climbed on foot, through the singing and dancing, to the Anglican monastery where I had found lodgings. I was moved by the joy of this whole people who had for twenty centuries prayed, "next year in Jerusalem" and who at last could pray "this year in Jerusalem."

I was also anxious for this people, because of the marriage vow its entire army was to take the next day, this solemn vow never to surrender the holy city. I met many soldiers, all very young; girl soldiers; children; astonishing characters in fur hats and long robes from the past that had at last been exorcised; and solid pioneers from the kibbutzim, with their horrible caps and tufts of hair sticking out from the top. Thousands of people were sleeping at the base of the walls, curled up like hunting dogs or stretched out facing the sky with their arms crossed over their chests.

The next day Israel, by parading her victorious troops, was going not only to defy the United Nations but also to take a very great risk of possible attack, of a grenade thrown into the stands, which might kill or wound hundreds of people.

An old Englishman who was living at the shelter of the Church of Christ told me: "No, monsieur, I will not go to that parade. It is a provocation. I shall do the same as all the members of all the diplomatic missions: I shall abstain. Besides, there will surely be an attack. Radio Damascus has said so."

But I was beginning to know the army of Israel and the men who commanded it—men who knew so well how to combine audacity with calculation. There would be no attacks the next day. Those who could have perpetrated them had already been killed or taken prisoner at Kuraiyima, in the course of a lightning raid on Jordanian territory.

Around 1:00 in the morning, after having broken radio silence to alert the military posts and patrols of our coming, we return to camp. Normally, the ambuscade would not have been terminated before daybreak, but tonight the frontier has been exceptionally calm. Perhaps they also think it better not to be encumbered too long with a guest of my sort. We come back by the same route, passing through the same ravines, following the same trail, taking the same precautions as on the way out. Once the ridge is crossed, the paratroopers snort like young horses; they begin to laugh and joke, lighting cigarettes and whistling through their teeth.

The sergeant asks me: "Were you at the May 2nd parade in Jerusalem? That really was something! I didn't march, but I was there on leave. What got the most applause? The flying formations or the tank columns? It was the paratroopers, wasn't it? There weren't very many of us; we had to guard the frontiers, keep our eye on al-Fatah. Those were buddies of mine who pulled off the raid on Kuraiyima. They knocked off more than 300 al-Fatah men and brought back 160. Often, it was done with a knife. It's because of Kuraiyima that the parade went off all right. Sure, one of the stands

*collapsed, but what a crazy idea it was to pile so many
people onto it! Al-Fatah should have claimed the credit!
Even so, it wasn't a bad show at all!"*

It was, indeed, a magnificent parade, from the Jaffa Gate
to the green and ocher hills of Romena. More than 800,000
people were massed along the route and in the stands. Among
the guests were representatives of all the big Jewish colonies
of the world. It was thus that I ran into H., whom I had met
in Mexico; V., whom I had known in Persia; and B., from
the United States. Their joy was naïve and exuberant. At
moments they gave the impression of having won the war
themselves, which did not fail to annoy the Israelis. The
soldiers of the Tsahal kept quiet. They knew that once more
they had achieved simply a single victory and that they would
have to continue training to win further battles, without ever
being done with the war.

I had found a place on the dais farthest away from the
officials, a dais for unimportant people: civil servants in the
Ministry of Foreign Affairs, former army captains and their
families, small tradesmen who had somehow managed to
make the pilgrimage from the ends of the earth to the Holy
Land. Five minutes before the start of the parade, scheduled
for 9:00, my neighbors climbed up on their bench, while
others brought out cameras or jostled one another. I asked
what was happening: "Ben-Gurion is here," someone said.
The intransigent old lion, emerged from his far-off kibbutz
in the Negev, had just arrived as the last and humblest of the
guests, without an escort and accompanied only by three or
four members of his kibbutz. But the Mayor Kolleck went to
join him. Moshe Dayan would have done so, too, had he not
been pinned down by his official role as Minister of Defense.
He was seated next to Prime Minister Levi Eshkol, who had
done his utmost to keep him out of that post.

I leaned forward and was able to catch a glimpse of a
stocky little man with a square face, white locks flowing in

all directions, and the features of a stubborn prophet baked by the desert sun. In the face of enormous difficulties he had created not only the State of Israel but also its army, which was born before the state itself. He is, what is more, a unique figure in the history of mankind.

He had exiled himself among us, the unimportant people. Was it not he himself who resigned from office, ostentatiously refusing all honors, because he is one of those men who cannot bear not to be first? My neighbor, a longtime Israeli ambassador in the East, murmured to me: "It is Ben-Gurion who ought to have been in the place of honor today; it is his army that won; it is the flag he designed that flies over all the rooftops. All the colonels and all the generals were appointed by him. He was always an impossible man, authoritarian, but without him Israel would never have existed, let alone its army. He had to impose his conception of warfare on a reluctant, if not downright rebellious, general staff. In 1948 the Haganah chiefs were convinced they would only have to fight bands of brigands and mercenaries, never regular armies with European equipment. The exact opposite happened. Israel was saved because Ben-Gurion moved heaven and earth to purchase heavy equipment—planes and tanks—secretly from abroad. His whole career, his whole life, is interwoven with that of this army that is going to parade. But everyone is waiting for him to die, so that they can erect the statues that he deserves. Alive he still exasperates everybody."

As in every parade, the presentation of the colors started things off. At the head fluttered the big star of David, emblem of the army of Israel, the Tsahal; the blue star on a white background was followed by the flags of all the services. Some of the emblems were made of iron, like the ensigns of the Roman legions and of the armored divisions of the Wehrmacht. Then came men of the paratroop reconnaissance unit, riding on jeeps, armed with 105 mm. recoilless rifles and Browning machine guns; these were the men who had opened the road across the dunes of Sinai for the Israeli armored brigades. They had jumped into minefields and attacked heavy tanks at point-blank range. They had gotten lost and found themselves behind the Egyptian lines, attacking without pause, on some nights covering more than forty miles and fighting all the way. It was they who had suffered the heaviest losses.

Then came motorized artillery in strange shape—chunks of battered scrap iron, one might say, some of which had been used in the Tripoli campaign in World War II; then followed French AMX light tanks, equipped with SS 10 and SS 11 rockets, the only modern equipment that the armored corps possessed. Behind them lumbered old Sherman and Patton tanks from the Normandy invasion and the heavy Centurions whose guns seemed to be made of two attached tubes secured by ring joints. They dated from 1943 or 1945 and had been bought for the price of the scrap iron—and then rebuilt or modified countless times since. The artillery consisted mostly of 120 mm. and 150 mm. mortars, self-propelled 105 mm. guns, 70 mm. Mark B antiaircraft guns, and a few American Hawk missiles.

This corps, which had just destroyed three Arab armies in six days, was almost entirely equipped with matériel that the Western countries had long since consigned to the scrap heap.

Then came the array of captured enemy equipment: armored troop carriers, amphibious tanks, enormous Stalin tanks and Soviet T 34, T 54 and T 55 tanks fitted out with infrared gun sights to make night firing possible. These recently manufactured tanks were very low and streamlined, with wide tracks. They were maneuverable, fast, and well armored. Next to them the old Israeli tanks seemed to belong to another century. Then came the SU 100s, the Jordanian Long Toms that had bombarded Tel Aviv, Katyusha rocket launchers, and two-stage SAM missiles. Once again, as I watched the modern armored equipment and artillery of the

Arabs roll past behind the old, worn-out Israeli matériel, I wondered by what miracle the Jews had won.

"Because of Yahweh, god of the armies," my neighbor the diplomat answered with a laugh.

More paratroopers came by, this time on foot, in close formation. They were thin and nervous, and several were out of step. They were the ones who had thrown themselves onto the Egyptian guns in the Sinai; those guns had been too powerful for the Israeli tanks and artillery to approach when they went on the offensive.

Next came part of the Golani brigade, one of the best and oldest infantry units of the Tsahal—the women's contingent, short skirts, caps cocked over one eye, Uzi submachine guns at their hips. The spectators clapped till their hands ached.

All at once, there was a great shout. From the four corners of the horizon Mirages, Mystères and Super Mystères swept across the sky, trailing streamers of blue smoke. They had been the great victors of the war. In four hours they had put all the Egyptian aircraft and air bases out of commission. These planes were of French manufacture. It was here, in Israel, that I finally learned to distinguish a Mirage from a Mystère, a Super Mystère from an Ouragan. My teacher was a twelve-year-old kid. He pranced up and down beside me, a veritable pocket encyclopedia of everything that flies in the air, of everything that rolls on tracks on the ground, of everything that moves, and of everyone who marches.

The huge crowd shouted its joy and its love for this army, which had just given the country both new frontiers and a magnificent victory. I wanted to see David Ben-Gurion's face, but I couldn't manage it.

From Masada to the Brink
of the Six-Day War

After Beersheba the real Negev Desert begins: stony gray expanses with dunes here and there, a land cracked like dry skin. Every six or eight miles there is a splotch of dark green, an oasis where water flows among orange trees, vines, and flowers: a kibbutz. This life-giving water, drawn from the Jordan River or the Lake of Tiberias, has also caused many deaths. Diversion of the Jordan's waters was one of the causes of the 1967 war. Past the kibbutz once again there is gray land, across which a few Bedouin wander with their black goats and balding camels. We are driving toward the kibbutz of Sede Boqer; there, in retirement, lives the man whose life is synonymous with the history of Israel and its army, David Ben-Gurion, who has often been called "the armed prophet."

For thirty years, from 1935 to 1965, he put all his strength into propelling Israel toward its destiny. It has been said of him, as of Churchill, that he was remarkable in war and crises but that he was not made for peace. David Grin, who later took the name Ben-Gurion in memory of one of the last defenders of Jerusalem against the Romans, was born on October 16, 1886, in the little town of Plonsk in Poland. Two-thirds of the town's inhabitants were Jews. His father, Victor Grin, was a lawyer who wore a frock coat and stiff collar and smoked cigarettes—a crime to the orthodox Jews of Plonsk, who denounced him to the tsarist police as a "reformist."

At an early age, young Ben-Gurion was already behaving like a rebel. He learned the Talmud and the Torah, in the Hebrew tradition, committing entire chapters to memory. But one day he had had enough, and then and there he gave up all religious practice. He was fifteen years old when he discovered another form of religion: Zionism. At sixteen, he left to study engineering in Warsaw because he knew that the future State of Israel would need technicians rather than merchants or lawyers. Already he was saying, "The Jewish people must obtain its rights in Palestine not by words but by deeds." He joined a socialist movement and stored weapons in his father's cellar. It was the time of the great pogroms. More than 150 Jewish communities were destroyed, and one of the Tsar's advisers declared, "A third of Russian Jews will be converted, a third will emigrate, and the rest will be exterminated."

BEN-GURION IN THE PROMISED LAND

At twenty, Ben-Gurion left for Palestine on an old Russian cargo boat that leaked all over. He wrote to his father:

In my view, the founding of a new village in Palestine is more important than a thousand congresses and a thousand conferences. The only, the true Zionism is the colonization of Palestine; all the rest is only foolishness, idle chatter, and a waste of time.

He had hardly arrived when he entered into a struggle with the rich Jewish landowners, who preferred to employ Arabs, rather than their own coreligionists, as day laborers. The Arabs were more robust, knew farm work, and demanded less money. Ben-Gurion became a farm worker himself and wandered from farm to farm, half-starving and dressed in rags. He was both a nationalist and a socialist.

Little by little, however, his socialism was to give way to his nationalism.

In Jerusalem, Ben-Gurion took up journalism and published a small newspaper, which had only 250 readers in Palestine and 100 abroad. When war broke out in 1914, the Turks expelled him along with many other activists. A red seal bearing the words "expelled forever from the confines of the Turkish Empire" was stamped on his passport. "I will come back," he declared.

Ben-Gurion and his friend Yitzhak Ben Zvi (who was to become the second President of the Republic of Israel) landed in New York in 1915, where Ben-Gurion married Paula, who was to be his faithful companion all her life. In his diary, which he kept scrupulously, we find this laconic account of the event: "New York, December 3 (1917): evening meeting of the Working Committee. December 4: meeting of our associations committees. December 5 at 11:30 A.M.: I am married. December 6: meeting of the Central Committee."

He enlisted in the British army and returned to Palestine as a corporal in the Royal Fusiliers, certainly the worst corporal in the entire British army. The war ended, but he continued to fight his personal war, taking long absences without informing his superiors.

He took part in numerous secret meetings, which, however, did not have to be secret. But that was part of the folklore that the Russian revolutionaries of 1905 bequeathed to Israel. Much of that heritage remains today: the taste for espionage and secrecy as well as division into all sorts of factions that excommunicate one another and hate one another ferociously. Corporal Ben-Gurion, who was by then hardly ever seen with his unit, was tried and reduced in rank, but this discipline did not seem to affect him. With some other comrades he founded the Histadrut, the General Confederation of Labor. This powerful organization, which soon became a state within the state, had only 4,000 members at that time. It was later to have 800,000. The great man of Zionism at that time was Dr. Chaim Weizmann. As compensation for his immense contribution to the Allied victory, through his discovery, among other things, of the acetone synthesis that made possible the continuous manufacture of munitions, Lord Balfour granted Weizmann what he most desired, a refuge for his persecuted countrymen in the very land of their ancestors. In November 1917 Balfour issued his celebrated declaration: "His Majesty's Government view with favor the establishment in Palestine of a national home for the Jewish people. . . ."

For thirty years the entire history of Zionism was interwoven with the conflict between Weizmann, the great scientist and friend of England, who was always disposed toward compromise, and Ben-Gurion, the stubborn, realistic little Polish Jew who was willing to make no concessions.

Ben-Gurion won because he is a "searchlight that beams all its power on a single point, leaving everything else in obscurity" (Michel Bar-Zohar, *Ben-Gurion: The Armed Prophet*, Englewood Cliffs, N.J.: Prentice-Hall). His single point was the creation of a Jewish state in Israel and not simply a "national home."

Ben-Gurion also insisted that the entire international Zionist movement be directed not by the foreign "moneybags," whom he scorned, but by the pioneers who were building Israel with their own hands.

THE SINGLE CHIEF OF ZIONISM

After succeeding Weizmann in 1935, Ben-Gurion became the effective chief of the entire Zionist apparatus. He was incredibly active, rushing ceaselessly around Palestine and the world, sometimes reading a book a day. A self-taught genius (he never finished his formal studies, or even really began them), Ben-Gurion devoured everything that came into his hands, no matter what the language. He already spoke Russian, Hebrew, German, and English. He learned Spanish to read Cervantes in the original and French to plunge into the memoirs of Marshal Foch. Later, when he became responsible for defense, he piled his desk high with everything written on the art of war: Clausewitz, Liddell Hart, Julius Caesar, Napoleon. He was attacked from both left and right without result: He has the hide of a crocodile. Ben-Gurion knew that a state could not exist without an army and that it was necessary first to create that army, the Haganah. Although many leaders wanted the illegal Haganah to function only as an organization of self-defense, Ben-Gurion insisted that it become a solid force, capable of attack and of imposing the Jewish state on its neighbors. Ben-Gurion entered into conflict with the other clandestine movements, like the Irgun and the Stern Gang, because they had their own armies and he wanted his to be the only one. Yet he also criticized the Haganah and its shock troops, the Palmach, because he considered their officers too pro-Soviet and he also wanted the army to be apolitical.

When on May 14, 1948, he proclaimed the State of Israel, becoming at once the first President of the Council and the first Minister of Defense, he had at his disposal 45,000 men and women equipped with light weapons. But his emissaries, aided by the "moneybags" in the United States, had already purchased heavy war matériel, artillery, and planes from various sources throughout the world. So when full-scale war broke out against the regular armies of Syria, Iraq, Jordan, Egypt and Lebanon, he was able to hold them in check and even to defeat them.

After long years as the all-powerful chief of Israel (even the word "dictator" was quite often applied to him), Ben-Gurion retains the ascetic tastes of his youth. In summer he wears a white shirt and trousers, in winter a dark suit, always with the shirt collar open. He pays no attention whatever to food. He is known to have hardly any friends. His irritable and violent character and his need to humiliate his adversaries have won him many enemies. They are to be found in every walk of life, from the extreme right to the extreme left, and even in the army. He was, indeed, forced to crush the resistance of officers accustomed to the loose discipline of the underground, and some have never forgiven him. On December 13, 1953, exhausted by this incessant struggle, he resigned from all his posts and left with Paula for the kibbutz of Sede Boqer, where he moved into a prefabricated wooden house. He still lives in the same cottage, and it is there that I am to meet him.

Moshe Dayan writes in his journal of the Sinai campaign, "For him the colonization of the Negev is the supreme expression of a revitalized Israel, changing the wild desert into a source of life, thanks to the courage of her new immigrants and young people born here who have left the comfort of the cities to participate in the adventures of the pioneers. The antithesis, in his eyes, is the city of Tel Aviv, and I have heard him murmur, as he walked through its crowded streets: 'Nineveh!' "

Nevertheless, his first retreat lasted only a short time. On February 21, 1955, in the wake of a dark espionage scandal which threw into question the very unity of the army—the army that he himself had created—Ben-Gurion again became Minister of Defense. In the Arab world an adversary as formidable as himself confronted him: Colonel Nasser. Immediately Ben-Gurion took the direction of "his" army back into his own hands, and in order to stifle internal quarrels, he instantly set it to fighting. On May 26 the Israelis launched a bloody reprisal raid on Gaza. Forty Egyptian soldiers were killed. Ben-Gurion does not believe in the Arab peace, in the U.N., in treaties or in conferences but only in force and determination.

Against him President of the Council Moshe Sharett did not carry much weight. Sharett was an astute and able man, but "the Old Man" did not spare him. Sharett wanted to negotiate with the Arabs, to outmaneuver them. Ben-Gurion sensed the danger and knew that war was coming.

The Russians became the protectors of the Arab world,

showering it with stocks of armaments. Israel was in danger
of being strangled. For the first time Nasser closed the Strait
of Tiran and the Gulf of 'Aqaba, blocking access to the Israeli
bridgehead of Elath and all the new state's maritime traffic
with Asia and Africa. He also barred the passage of Israeli
shipping in the Suez Canal. The test of strength was ap-
proaching. Ben-Gurion got rid of Sharett, who did not want
war with Egypt. He himself took over the post of President
of the Council, he made Moshe Dayan Chief of Staff, and
together they drew up plans for invasion of the Sinai. The
nationalization of the Suez Canal precipitated Franco-
British intervention. France became the principal supplier of
arms to Israel.

French and British paratroopers jumped over Suez. Egyptian airfields were bombed, and Moshe Dayan's armored
brigades fanned out across the Sinai Desert. Egypt collapsed.
But Nasser knew how to transform this defeat into a victory,
thanks to the support of the Russians and the Americans. The
British and the French evacuated the Suez Canal. Ben-
Gurion, in turn, had to capitulate, and his army, which had
conquered the Sinai, was forced to withdraw to its original
positions. Ben-Gurion later told a group of officers, very
sadly: "You conquered the Sinai; I retreated from it." An
attack on him with a grenade in the Knesset, the Israeli parliament, nearly cost him his life. He was wounded, along
with several ministers, but he shouted, "Stay in your seats!"

Ben-Gurion was old and tired; once again he had to give
up power. On July 16, 1963, consumed with bitterness, he
retired finally to Sede Boqer. The Israelis were quite willing
to keep him around, like a flag or a statue. But his comrades
in arms and especially the younger generation had drifted
away from him. He tried to regain power in the elections of
1965 but failed. He was openly denounced as a liar, a dictator, an unbalanced personality. The state of Israel, though
still very young, can show ingratitude every bit as well as its
elders.

But before the Six-Day War broke out, during the three weeks of anguish that preceded it, when Chief of Staff Rabin was suffering from nervous depression and Prime Minister Levi Eshkol was spouting nonsense on the radio, the people remembered Ben-Gurion. It was his lieutenant, Moshe Dayan, whom the army and public opinion forced upon the Ministry of Defense. Before accepting, Dayan sent an emissary to Ben-Gurion.

"Is Moshe sure of himself?" the old man asked.

"Yes."

"In that case give him my blessing" (Bar-Zohar, *Histoire sociale de la guerre d'Israël*, Paris: Fayard).

THE HISTORY OF ISRAEL

AS TOLD BY DAVID BEN-GURION

The kibbutz of Sede Boqer, like many desert kibbutzim, is filled with flowers. I am led along a walk lined with bright red hollyhocks to the "old lion's" small wooden house. He is there in his office, his eyes lively and shrewd, his nose strong, his body squat and round; his belt rides up on his stomach over a khaki shirt with pockets. His white hair, which once formed a kind of halo, is mostly gone. Only his temples are still not bare. He will soon be eighty-two years old. His faithful companion Paula is dead. Surrounded by books in every language, he is working on a manuscript. His memoirs? Probably. They should be a great settling of accounts, for age has not in the least robbed him of his virulence or softened his grudges. He raises his head and asks me, in that dry voice of his, stressing the last words, "What do you want of me?"

"That you tell me about the army of Israel."

A gleam of tenderness comes into his eyes. I've been warned: "The Old Man" may very well keep me no more than three minutes and blithely send me packing if he

*doesn't recall my face or if my first question displeases him.
But in bringing up the army I have him hooked.*

*Ben-Gurion takes off his spectacles, and in a familiar ges-
ture begins to pound the table with little blows of his fist.
He speaks in French, in English, sometimes in Hebrew. My
guide then translates for me, but when "The Old Man"
doesn't like the translation or finds it imprecise he gets
angry, with the passion of a young man.*

*"When I created that army I had two aims. The first was
the defense of Israel. The Arab countries had all rejected the
U.N. partition plan, and it was urgent to face up to this
threat. The second, just as important as the first, was to
create a Jewish nation, which did not exist, any more than
a Jewish people existed. It's about this, above all, that I'll
tell you. Do you know the history of the Jews?"*

"No, of course not."

*"All right, then, we'll have a little history before we get to
the problem that interests you.*

*"In the course of the Diaspora, which lasted 2,000 years,
the Jews were scattered all around the world. They were
forcibly subjected to the political and economic influences
of the countries in which they lived. In the Middle Ages,
civilization was Arabic, and the Jews who lived in contact
with the Arabs were among the most civilized of peoples.
This was the case of the Jews in Moorish Spain. Europe
took up the banner as the Arab culture declined. The western
Jews thus profited in their turn from this shift in civilization.*

*"At the beginning of the eighteenth century there were
2.5 million Jews in the world, 1.5 million eastern Jews, 1 million western Jews. At the end of the nineteenth century,
thanks to good living conditions in Europe, western Jews
constituted 88 percent of the Jewish people.*

*"The eastern Jews continued to pray three times a day,
asking for their return to the promised land, but they left to
God, to Adonai, the job of arranging the operation. They
did not think to bring it about themselves. The western Jews,*

*thanks to the realistic influences to which they were sub-
jected, began to think in a different way: For heaven to help
you, you must help yourself.*

"*The French Revolution, with its slogan Liberté, Égalité,
Fraternité, had a tremendous impact on all the Jews of
Europe. It was in France, where the Jews were best assim-
ilated, that Crémieux, Minister of Justice under Gambetta,
created the Alliance Israelite Universelle [Universal Jewish
Alliance]. His aim was to reunite the people of the Diaspora
in their own country. The Alliance sent an emissary to
Palestine to see what could be done. That emissary found
four Jewish colonies, all established in cities: at Jerusalem,
Hebron, Safad and Tiberias. The name of that emissary was
Charles Netter. He understood at once that the Jews could
not stay in the cities if they wanted to rediscover their homeland but would have to devote themselves to agriculture
and become pioneers. Netter went to see the Sultan in
Istanbul and obtained from him a ninety-nine-year lease on
the undistributed virgin lands of Palestine. That was in 1870.
It was not until 1878 that the first farm village was created,
with colonists trained in an agricultural school founded by
Netter. Other farm villages began to take root. What had
been considered impossible—Jewish pioneers—became a
reality. Today Israel is the country with the most advanced
agriculture after Japan.*

"*Next it was necessary to create a language. In general,
the Jews spoke the languages of the countries they lived in.
Sixty-two years ago, when I arrived in Jerusalem, the Jews
were using forty different dialects. Today, 700,000 students
study in Hebrew in all the schools of Israel. And they said it
was impossible to bring a dead language back to life!*

"*After World War I immigrants came from Europe. After
World War II they came especially from Asia and Africa.
These immigrants were poor and underdeveloped. Enormous
differences existed between eastern Jews and western Jews.
To make Israel one nation it was necessary to reduce that*

difference at all costs. Only one means existed: the army. Only the army was capable of assimilating men who belonged to different worlds, separated by several centuries of civilization. The army was the melting pot of the Israeli nation. It made it possible to raise the living standard of the poorest people, to make them equal citizens like the others. Our miracle could succeed—and can succeed—only thanks to the army and within its ranks. We dressed these recent arrivals exactly like the sabras born in Israel of parents from Europe. We made them study in the same way; we fed them the same food. Many eastern Jews had never been to primary school, in spite of the laws obliging their parents to send them. The army was thus transformed into a huge school. When I was Minister of Defense I decided that every soldier who was a recent immigrant must spend at least six months in school in order to reach a certain level of education. Thanks to the army, we instilled in this people, who loved anarchy and factionalism, a sense of nationality, the taste and desire to fight in defense of their country. If we have succeeded in defeating the Arab countries in three successive wars, it is because we have managed to instill this sense of nationality in all our people. The earlier arrivals had it; the new arrivals acquired it. We all know why we are fighting, whereas the Egyptians are always asking themselves, when war breaks out, what on earth they are doing in the Sinai. With the Egyptians, the first ones to run away are the officers. With us, the first to die are the officers. In our army, the command 'Forward' does not exist; it has been replaced by another command, which the officers shout in the moment of attack: 'Follow me!'

"Discipline in our army, despite appearances, is extremely tough. But we have found a form of relationship between the soldiers and their officers quite different from everywhere else. It is based on a deep feeling of equality. At the beginning of the creation of the army in Israel, at the time of the Haganah and the underground, discipline was non-existent. The members were all volunteers who only wanted to follow

their own inclinations. It was not easy to instill a sense of discipline in them. We had a very hard time.

"We were able to obtain a measure of discipline the moment the officers finally understood that their soldiers would never believe in them unless they themselves set the examples. This is why, in spite of the very tough discipline of the Israeli army, relations have always remained very friendly between officers and soldiers.

"I also wanted this army to be young. I knew that there were big risks involved in entrusting important commands to very young commanders. But isn't it even more dangerous to entrust them to old men who live by ancient notions of tactics and continually hark back to outdated military history? Of the six chiefs of staff I appointed, not a single one was over forty. The chiefs today are older, but the army, fortunately, has remained astonishingly young.

"The best unit of the Haganah was the Palmach, half of whose members came from kibbutzim. They were all volunteers for one year or two. For two weeks they trained, and for another two weeks they worked in the fields to feed themselves. They learned to know their country with their feet. They crossed it in every direction. It was truly an excellent unit, from which one could create the nucleus of an army. The Palmach was however only a shock battalion equipped with light arms. We needed trucks, tanks, and planes right away. The real shock troops would be the tankers, the flyers, the paratroopers. The Palmach then ceased to be the elite unit, though it refused for a long time to believe it. But it was with its cadres that we shaped the new army of Israel. Today, any foot soldier of any infantry regiment is better than the best of the Palmach soldiers."

I ask, "Will Israel have to return the territories that it occupied during the Six-Day War?"

I have put this question to all the generals of the Israeli army. Ben-Gurion narrows his eyes. Have I suddenly awakened his mistrust? At last he replies:

"It is an ordinary citizen who answers you. If I had to

choose only between peace and liberty, I would choose liberty, and I would say that we must hold onto the occupied territories. But I prize both peace and liberty. Only, for me, peace is not just a piece of paper that you sign and then tear up; it is the amicable bonds created between two countries, the will to cooperate together in all areas: cultural, political, and economic. Today, because of the present Arab leaders, this peace does not seem possible to me. There is thus no choice: We hold onto the occupied territories. The Middle East is in perpetual ferment. Peace will be made only with the support of the great powers—Europe, Russia, and America. But, although the Russians and the Americans do not want war, they mistrust each other. Only Europe can bring us peace, but a reunited Europe. It would then be the balancing factor that would bring Russia and America together. A Soviet ambassador in Israel said to me, 'The greatest danger for Russia is not America, but China.' This obsession with China can bring the Russians and Americans together and make them more liberal. When Stalin was in power, the lie was in power. Today every Russian knows that his standard of living is lower than that of the European countries or the United States, and he wants to attain that higher standard of living. It's not by waging war that he will get there."

We leave the little air-conditioned room. Ben-Gurion walks a few steps with me among the roses. I ask him: "Do you know that Arab journalists write that they, the Arabs, are the Vietcong and the Jews in the Middle East are the American imperialists? The Israeli journalists say the opposite."

Ben-Gurion halts. "That reminds me of a story. It was in the month of August 1946 in Paris. I was having serious difficulties then with the British, who wanted to have me arrested. I had taken refuge in France. I had found lodgings in the Hotel Monceau. When I arrived, a wide red carpet was stretched from the entrance up the stairs to the room of

*a guest of honor of the French government. That guest was
Ho Chi Minh. We met almost every evening and discussed
our problems at length. His relations with the French government seemed to be deteriorating, for as the days passed
the carpet grew shorter and shorter. One day, there was no
more carpet there at all. I asked Ho Chi Minh then, 'Things
are no longer going very well, eh?'*

" 'No,' he told me. 'And with you?'

" 'With me things are going very badly too.'

*"Then he made me a strange proposition: 'The negotiations
have broken down; I am going back to Vietnam. I propose
that you leave with me and set up your government in exile
there.'*

*"I thanked him, but I made it clear to him that I couldn't
accept."*

*Ben-Gurion passes a hand over his skull and plunges it
back into his pocket; then he sticks out his stomach under
his khaki shirt: "No, really, it is we who are the Vietcong.
We are fighting to defend our country against men who
mostly think about defending their positions and their financial privileges."*

*With short steps, Ben-Gurion goes back inside his cottage.
An armed sentinel concealed behind a hedge is already keeping watch over him, as over an official monument.*

*Yet how much life, how much energy still pulse in this
man whom nothing could break!*

One day, a long time ago, he said to Shimon Peres, who
was to become his Deputy Minister of Defense: "You know,
Trotsky was not a statesman. At Brest-Litovsk he said
'neither war nor peace.' That was no good. He should have
decided, settled the question: either war or peace. He was
not like Lenin, who said: 'peace!' It was because Trotsky was
not a true Russian—because he was a Jew—that he was not
a statesman. He didn't understand; he didn't grasp the profound truths of Soviet Russia. . . ."

No one sensed and understood the profound truths of Israel as the "old lion" did. He molded this country and this army in his own image. If Israel sometimes resembles Sparta, it is because it resembles Ben-Gurion.

One cannot explain the Israeli army without speaking of Ben-Gurion, its creator. One cannot understand it—for it is different from all other armies—without knowing its history. Born in the underground, it has retained certain characteristics of the underground.

SOLDIERS OF THE BIBLE

But first I would like to reestablish one historical truth and to destroy a legend—that of the Jew as bad soldier, incapable of bearing arms. The entire ancient history of Israel, as the Bible tells us, was primarily a military history. The soldiers of Moses, of Joshua, and of David never stopped fighting and even quarreling among themselves. They were not gentle with their vanquished enemies. In the Bible there are innumerable tales of populations put to the sword, of cities razed to the ground, of tribes driven into exile. If the victors spared women it was because they were virgins and could serve. Jehovah, the God of Israel, was also the god of armies, a rude warrior who led, with great harshness, his undisciplined people, who were tempted by every novelty. The Jews fought Assyrians, Babylonians, Egyptians, Canaanites, Moabites, Ammonites, Persians, Greeks, and Romans, in turn. Defeated by the legions of Titus after desperate struggle, they chose to put themselves to the sword at Masada rather than to surrender.

When the Romans were preparing to attack the old citadel of Herod overlooking the Dead Sea, the chief of the Jewish resistance fighters, Eleazar Ben-Yair, made this speech to his companions: Let us make haste to destroy the Romans' hope of triumphing over us, and may their amazement at being able to vent their rage only on dead bodies force them to admire our courage.

Flavius Josephus gives us this account of the end of the Jewish Zealots:

They embraced their wives and their children, tearfully bade them their last goodbyes, gave them their last kisses; and then, as if they had borrowed the hands of strangers, they executed that fatal resolve, representing in themselves the necessity that constrained them thus to snatch out their own hearts in snatching life from them in order to deliver them from the outrages that their enemies would have made them suffer. Not one of them quailed before so tragic a deed; all killed their wives and their children; and, convinced as they were that the state to which they had been reduced obliged them to do it, they considered this horrible carnage as the least of the evils that they had to fear. . . . Then each man flung himself on the corpses of his nearest and dearest, and, embracing them, bared his throat to those who had been picked for this hideous office. They accomplished their task without betraying the slightest horror of it. . . .
The Romans, beholding this vast number of corpses, instead of rejoicing, considering them as enemies, could not tire of admiring how, through so great a scorn for death, so many people had conceived and executed so strange a resolve.

In the heroic decision of the defenders of Masada, modern Israel has found the symbol of its own will—preferring death to servile existence. Across the centuries of passivity and resignation, the young Israelis have rediscovered the spirit that animated Eleazar Ben-Yair. And today recruits in the armored units of the Israeli defense forces take their oath of obedience on the summit of Masada, repeating the words of a modern Hebrew poet: "Never again will Masada fall."

AND EVEN MERCENARIES

After Titus's destruction of the temple of Jerusalem, the fall of Masada, and the suppression of Bar Kochba's revolt, the Diaspora began. From this period on Jewish mercenaries were to be found in almost all the armies of the Mediterranean basin. Corps of Jewish mercenaries served with the Egyptian Ptolemys and the Seleucids in Persia. Antiochus III, the Great, satrap of Lydia, wrote: "I have decided to pull 2,000 Jewish families with their household effects out of Mesopotamia and Babylon, in order to send them to the most important garrisons and positions. . . . My ancestors attested to their fidelity and their prompt obedience to orders."

The Romans continued, even after A.D. 70, to enroll Jews in their legions. These mercenaries very often formed military colonies like that of the Zamarids. By the end of the fourth century, Jewish soldiers in the Roman army were so numerous that the fathers of the Church took alarm. They even managed to obtain an edict forbidding Jews to bear arms. This law was very loosely applied, so greatly were the Jewish soldiers appreciated. They even had certain privileges like, for example, exemption from service on the Sabbath and the right to eat food prepared in accordance with their rites —that is, kosher food.

Later, they fought alongside the Persians in the war against Byzantium. On the fringes of the Sahara there were some extremely warlike Jewish tribes who even founded a sort of Saharan empire around the town of Tamentit [Algeria]. It was a Jew, la-Kahena, who led an army of Christians, Berbers, and Jews against the Islamic invasion in the seventh century. In twelfth-century Spain, at the time of the *Reconquista*, Jews fought on both sides.

The Crusades marked a turning point; in the eleventh century a decree prohibited Jews from bearing arms in those holy wars. The ghetto era began, and with it another form of combat for all Jews.

In the West, in the twentieth century, Jews fought courageously in the armies of their respective countries. One example: Of the 600,000 Jews in Germany during World War I, 100,000 served as combat troops; 12,000 were killed, 35,000 decorated, and 2,000 commissioned from the ranks.

THE WATCHMEN AND THE GUARDIANS

Between 1870 and 1880 the first Jewish agricultural colonies in Palestine were founded, mostly in unhealthy places, by washed-out-looking men who knew nothing about farming. The Arabs called them the "sons of death." Indeed, were they not sons of death, these unarmed men from distant Europe, driven only by an incomprehensible mysticism to settle in Palestine?

The first pioneers had hardly arrived when they had to learn to protect themselves from the Bedouin. These pillagers attacked not only the Jews, but all other farmers, whether Moslem or Christian, as well. To forestall these raids the pioneers would assign two or three of their number as watchmen. These watchmen were the forerunners of the tank crews of Moshe Dayan's armored divisions. At that time, a typical Jewish colony would be composed of a few wooden barracks forming a square, like the Saharan *bordjes* (isolated clockhouses), surrounded by dried-mud walls. These colonists raised a few hundred sheep and some horses and tilled the stony fields.

On the Sabbath, the Jews might be praying in their rudimentary synagogue. Suddenly there would be a whirlwind of sand and shouts. The watchman would burst into the synagogue; "The Bedouin!" All the men would rush out. They had no rifles, only knives and clubs. Usually there was the kind of old-fashioned free-for-all in which insults are as common as blows. There were no deaths, just cuts and bruises. Most often the Bedouin rode away without capturing any sheep, but sometimes they might drive a whole stolen flock before them. The authorities did nothing. In the Turkish Empire "authorities" no longer existed. The only relations were the relations of force, respect, or hatred that linked mounted Bedouin brigands and the Jewish colonists with their romantic thirst.

The Jews did not display much solidarity. They founded colonies that were isolated, very different, and sometimes hostile toward one another. Between a Yemenite Jew and a western Jew saturated with Russian socialism hardly any point of contact existed. Near Tel Aviv there was a colony that bore the very beautiful name of Petah Tiqwa—"the gate of hope." It was inhabited by eastern Jews. Its policeman and night watchman, "Shomrier" Abraham Shapira, was as celebrated for his strength and courage among the Bedouin as among the Jews. One day Shapira learned that the Bedouin had stolen horses from a nearby colony of Russian Jews. He immediately went to see the sheik, who received him, as usual, with the greatest respect. Shapira reproached him for having stolen the horses.

"I don't understand you," the sheik replied. "You guard the colony of Petah Tiqwa. Because it is you who guard it, we respect it. We steal only from the Jews who come from Europe. I fail to see what you can object to, you who are my brother and who speak Arabic. You are not of their kind. It has nothing to do with you."

Although certain colonies had their own guards, like Shapira, others preferred to buy the services of neighboring sheiks. They paid a fee to live in peace. This practice of "baksheesh" ended by saddling the Jewish villages with regular Arab or Bedouin overlords, who exacted heavier and heavier tributes. The dissension between eastern and western Jews went so far that some eastern Jews, generally more puritanical, even sent their Arab "protectors" to attack a colony of Russian Jews who had shockingly permitted themselves to stage a concert.

In 1907 and 1908, after the great pogroms in Russia and Poland, a large number of western Jews arrived in Palestine; hardened by their own experience, they insisted that Jews could be defended only by other Jews. A secret organization, the Hachomer, was founded; its purpose was to defend the lives, property, and honor of all Jews, regardless of where they came from. It took as its motto "In blood and fire, Judah fell: in blood and fire, Judah will rise again."

The notion of honor was a novel one to the Jews of the Diaspora. It resulted from a genuine revolution in outlook. The Jew of the Diaspora wanted only to survive, bowing his head until the wave passed by. In Israel he suddenly learned, in the name of honor, to hold his head up. There Jews soon became again that "stiff-necked" people of whom Jehovah was already complaining in the time of Moses. They ceased to be the sons of death, who could be massacred without fear of retribution. And so the members of the Hachomer, "the guardians," would risk their lives for a stolen bunch of grapes, that is, for the sake of honor. At first there were ten guardians, and they possessed among them one rifle, one six-shooter, and one Circassian dagger. To impress the Arabs they deliberately chose a dazzling uniform, but it was not until 1910 that they obtained horses and boots. Soon, for twenty farm colonies, there were 150 guards; but numbers were less important than the symbol.

In Europe and in Russia, among all the Jews threatened by pogroms, the exploits of the Hachomer took on the dimensions of legend. Israel became, for all the young people, not the land of the Bible, where one went to die, but the land of hope, of liberty, the land where Jews had weapons, rode on horseback—and held up their heads.

Shortly before World War I the Hachomer expanded its role of guarding existing colonies and began to found new colonies of a quasi-military type, already foreshadowing the present-day Nahal.

The Hachomer guardian, arrogant astride his magnificent horse in his braid-encrusted uniform and Circassian cap or Bedouin kaffiyeh, cartridge belts crossed on his chest and long sword at his side, impetuous and impatient, was already advertising that the wandering Jew had come home at last, that the prodigal children of Israel had returned to leave no more.

BIRTH OF AN ARMY

Then World War I broke out. At the beginning the situation of the Palestinian Jews was far from simple: As a minority in the Ottoman Empire they were under pressure to line up on thé German side. But Turkish oppression on one hand and French aid on the other (aid that made possible, among other things, the development of the colonies and the Hachomer) pushed them toward the Allies. Then a wild hope was born: If the German camp were to lose the war, perhaps a Jewish state could come into being. Turkish repression—arrests and expulsions, which decimated the Hachomer—put an end to hesitation: Aside from a timid minority who collaborated more or less openly with the Turkish occupation out of fear of repression, the future Israelis swung over to the Franco-British side.

Two kinds of resistance immediately developed: internally and underground, in which the Israeli apprenticeship in secrecy and terrorism began, and externally, participation in the British army. One man, the first military figure of the Israeli army, soon stood out: Joseph Trumpeldor, a hero of the Russo-Japanese War, in which he had lost an arm but had won an officer's stripes. An immigrant to Palestine in 1912 and the shining symbol of the Israeli farmer-soldier, he declared to his fellow Jews, those who had, like him, been exiled by the Turks, as well as those in the Diaspora:

We Jews now have the opportunity to fight with our own hands to liberate our country and to build a homeland anew. We have the opportunity to show the world that, if we are given the chance, we are capable of fighting with strength and sacrifice, even more than other peoples, for we need a country in which we can live like normal people. We have no other country than Israel, to which we are attached by the bond of a brilliant past, and we want to construct a homeland on just foundations.

After his expulsion from Palestine in 1914, Trumpeldor met in Egypt another heroic figure of Zionist resistance: Zecw Jobotinski. Both of them quickly came to the same conclusion: As a reward for the wartime assistance to the Allies, the Jews would later be able to claim the right to part of the conquered territory, notably Palestine. Their idea of a Jewish army was, however, premature: The British government would permit the creation of only one service-and-supply batallion, the "Zion Mule Corps." This was only a small step forward. The first "Israeli" regular soldier was distinguished from a British private only by a blue-and-white shoulder patch marked with the shield of David.

The second step, and it was a very important one, was taken by Chaim Weizmann in London, when in 1917 he obtained from Lord Balfour the famous declaration that "His Majesty's Government view with favour the establishment in Palestine of a national home for the Jewish people and will use their best endeavours to facilitate the achievement of this object . . ." At the same time, the formation of a Jewish legion was authorized. This legion, however, a regiment of three batallions in which a certain number of volunteers like Ben-Gurion enlisted, marked time in Egypt. The British dragged out its training, as well as the process of equipping it. Only two companies were even sent into combat.

A year later, Trumpeldor extracted from Kerensky in Moscow an authorization to mobilize 120,000 Russian Jews. Only the October Revolution prevented such a force from attacking the Turks by way of Armenia and invading Turkish Palestine.

After the cessation of hostilities the Jewish legion was exiled to the Sinai, where it was prevented even from going to the rescue of Jews harassed by a new outbreak of Arab terrorism. It became apparent that the British government would never tolerate the existence of a Jewish army. In fact, it proved to be just as hostile as the Turkish administration—

but more effective. Only one course remained for the Jews: to go underground. The Jewish soldiers, officially demobilized, "remobilized" themselves as shock commandos and intervened to protect the colonists when a series of pogroms swept Palestine in 1920 and 1921.

Britain, for fear of alienating the Arabs, refused to countenance this clandestine military force and organized severe repression. Arrests and imprisonments followed, provoking still greater irritation among the Jews and encouraging the spirit of secret resistance that is at the root of both the unique character and the strength of the Israeli army.

Arthur Koestler speaks of the phenomenon of the "white Negro," in connection with relations between the British administration and the Jewish defense organization, meaning that the latter changed its "color" according to the political situation. Although repression was the dominant British tactic, in view of the severe dangers faced by the Jews, the authorities occasionally tolerated for brief moments this clandestine and ever more popular army. Everybody was mobilized to assist it, from children to women to old men.

THE HAGANAH

In 1921 this army took the name of Haganah (the Resistance). Caught between illegality and the imperatives of self-defense, the Haganah was built, shaped, and trained during the eight years of calm that followed World War I.

On August 13, 1929, there was a new outburst of violence: The Grand Mufti of Jerusalem, Hajj Amin al-Husseini, preached a holy war, a *jihad*, claiming that the Jews had returned to Palestine to erect the Third Temple on the site of the mosque of Omar. The Arabs attacked the Jews everywhere at once in an outbreak that lasted seventy-three weeks. The rural colonies protected by the Haganah brilliantly resisted the Arab attacks (even though British troops had tried to confiscate their weapons on the eve of the conflict), while the communities of Hebron and Safad, which were under British protection, were wiped out.

Then Jews knew seven more years of peace, during which the Haganah found its vocation in the pioneer spirit. It was the great period of the defensive wall and the tower that Arthur Koestler describes in *Promise and Fulfilment:*

The process of founding new "points"—collective settlements— in insecure areas was developed by Haganah into a stereotyped routine. At night Haganah detachments occupied the "point"— generally a stony hill in the desert which had seen no plough since Biblical times. At dawn a convoy of lorries would arrive with prefabricated stockades, prefabricated living huts, plumbing, shower-bath and kitchen equipment ready for assembly; and, travelling on a caterpillar carrier, the centre of the new settle- ment: the watch-tower, with its searchlight whose cyclopic eye was to survey the surrounding terrain and send its twinkling signals to the nearest settlement ten or more miles away.

In October 1936 the Haganah established its first intelli- gence service. Its goal was to seek out and identify Arab terrorist gangs and to plan the tactics of the shock units.

Everything was clandestine; everything was illegal. A Jew caught carrying arms risked a sentence of ten years in prison from the British tribunals; if his weapon was loaded, the sentence was death. Smuggling weapons became an obliga- tion. What could not be purchased was manufactured on the spot: grenades, rifle grenades, mines, and explosive charges, which took the place of a nonexistent artillery and exploded whenever they felt like it. The weapons were buried under the kibbutzim—which posed problems. It became necessary to invent detonators that would not deteriorate in the damp.

Training was conducted at night, disguised as sporting- club outings on Mount Carmel or the shores of the Dead Sea near Masada. Pistols were transported in water canteens with false bottoms and grenades in loaves of bread.

Throughout, the Zionist leaders displayed an intelligence that was as cool on the surface as it was humane underneath:

"We must respond not with vengeance or aggression," they declared in one order of the day, "but by stepping up our constructive work. For each of our fallen comrades let us establish a new collectivist colony. Rather than evacuating the positions we hold, let us conquer another stretch of desert, drain a new swamp, and found new villages in Israel." Curiously enough, because of the Arab troubles, which continued without letup between 1936 and 1939, the Haganah was able to take a first step toward legal recognition. The British authorities, worried about their own security, created a rural police force in cooperation with the Jewish Agency— a police force whose sergeants (like Moshe Dayan) were then able to train and organize the secret army scattered in the villages and in the deserts.

Havlagah ("moderation") was the watchword of the Haganah. The British, disturbed by German and Italian penetration of the Arab world, provisionally came to terms with the Jews. They even went so far as to assign a Jewish interpreter to each British unit—a real bond of unity between the two armies. Better still, the Jews discovered in the person of a British officer their Lawrence of Palestine. He was Captain Orde Wingate, and he landed in Israel at the end of 1937.

He was an original spirit, a highly unusual person of an absolute nonconformity. The son of a minister and a great reader of the Bible, he spoke and read Hebrew. It was fashionable in the British army to be pro-Arab; he was pro-Zionist. He arrived in 1937 and departed a year and a half later, having left his mark for all time on the Haganah and the army that subsequently grew out of it.

He was the first person to show the Jews that they could be excellent soldiers without necessarily being imprisoned in the rigid codes of traditional armies. He taught them to fight at night because at night the Arab is afraid. He insisted that they get to know their country by night because a countryside is not the same in daylight as in darkness. Under cover of training the Jewish auxiliary police force, he created the "midnight battalions," the first regular units of the Haganah.

His Zionism quickly made him undesirable to the British, and he was obliged to leave Palestine. He went on to become the great hero of Burma in World War II. Thanks to his unconventional methods, which he had demonstrated with the Jews, he accomplished one of the greatest exploits of the war by creating a whole army of "Chindits" in the jungle behind the Japanese lines. He died futilely in a plane crash in 1944. The Israelis exalted his memory with deep gratitude and said of him, "If he had not died, he would have been the first chief of our army."

In 1939 the Haganah created a permanent special force composed of 600 young men organized into commando units —the Palmach, from which all the chiefs of the present army of Israel were graduated.

But in 1938 a dissident group had been formed among the most activist elements, which found the Haganah too patient and prudent. It preached terrorism, the struggle against the British as well as the Arabs, and the creation of a great Jewish state that would extend along both banks of the Jordan. Three thousand men from among the toughest elements of the Haganah enlisted under the banner of the Irgun. Even before it was officially born, the army of Israel had thus suffered its first schism.

The rise of Nazism and then its seizure of power in Germany precipitated a great flood of immigration, which exasperated the Arabs and therefore worried the British. The almost cordial Anglo-Jewish entente was finished. The period of hostilities began with the publication of a White Paper.

THE WHITE PAPER (1939–1945)

The White Paper added up, roughly, to a Draconian restriction of Jewish immigration and colonization of lands in Palestine. Only 75,000 Jews were to be allowed to enter

Palestine in the next five years. This restriction was accompanied by a curious clause: "unless the Arabs agree to let more come in." The Jewish population of Palestine was never to exceed one-third of the Arab population. That was in 1939; 6 million Jews in Poland, Russia, France, Holland, Germany, in fact all over Europe—6 million Jews were living their lives from day to day in the shadow of the ovens.

The emotion aroused by the publication of the White Paper was intense. From Jerusalem to Tel Aviv there was total bewilderment. But then the war broke out, and Britain itself led the struggle against Hitlerism. Dr. Weizmann, known for his British sympathies, went into eclipse. David Ben-Gurion suceeded him. He found a solution: "We shall fight the White Paper as if there were no war. We shall fight the war as if there had been no White Paper."

On the Arab side, nobody bothered to hide his sympathies for the Axis, whether it was Rashid Ali al-Ghailani in Iraq, Aziz Ali al-Masri in Egypt, or the eternal Mufti of Jerusalem. These antipathetic stands did not shake the British government, whose military tribunals in Palestine sent every Jew convicted of possessing arms to jail. Wingate's midnight commandos, among others, were the victims of British police repression; one small unit, voluntarily attached to the British army, was arrested in the middle of a training exercise and imprisoned on the spot. At the same time, all over Europe, underground networks were organized to enable the persecuted Jews to reach the promised land that Great Britain denied them.

Hitler's success did, however, modify Anglo-Israeli relations. The Arabs more and more openly announced themselves in favor of the Nazis and in 1941 proclaimed in Baghdad a holy war against the British. The latter were reduced to accepting the Jews as allies. There followed a series of farcical episodes in which white became black and black white: Jews were sentenced to years in prison for carrying arms or clandestine activities but released the next day.

The policy of "truces" continued. Most of the Irgun leaders, imprisoned in a camp at Latrun, were freed to take part in raids on Arab territory. Their chief, David Raziel, was killed in an air raid; he was buried with military honors by the British only a few months after having been sentenced to ten years in prison for terrorism.

Similarly, Moshe Dayan left a cell in St. John of Acre to lead the Jewish commandos. He fought alongside the Free French forces against the troops still loyal to Pétain in Syria. He lost an eye there, but he ensured his future popularity and earned his nickname of the "Jewish Scipio," not only in the Middle East, but also in central Europe (where Zionist paratroops landed to organize resistance) and in Italy, where the Jewish brigade landed with the Allies. Members of the Haganah were everywhere. Despite the White Paper, 30,000 Jews enlisted in the British army. Because of the White Paper, only 9,000 Arabs followed their example, and even then only after an intensive propaganda campaign.

The Haganah continued to grow through innumerable crises which, paradoxically, proved beneficial to it. No one will ever be able to say how much the Israeli army owes to Marshal Rommel, whose victorious Afrika Korps forced a truce between the British and the Jewish Agency. The truce was serious enough for the British to stifle their reluctance and set themselves to train the Jews in guerilla warfare and clandestine operations.

But unity did not reign in the embryonic army. Although the Irgun, for imperative reasons of survival, had provisionally joined the fragile Haganah-British coalition, a new terrorist group was born: the "fighters for Israeli freedom," better known as the Stern Gang. Its fanatical members had no intention of observing any truce; blind terrorism seemed to them the only valid course for eliminating all the enemies of Israel. Their exploits, both their raids and their escapes, quickly made them conspicuous. Whereas the Irgun had attacked British property, the Stern Gang aimed at people.

It became widely known after a particularly spectacular outrage: the assassination in Cairo, in October, of the resident
British Minister in the Middle East, Lord Moyne. Although
the assassins, two young men less than twenty years old,
were promptly hanged, the Zionist authorities, particularly
the Jewish Agency and the Haganah, fearing a revulsion of
international public opinion, which had up to then been
favorable to Israel, decided to put a stop to the Stern Gang.
Unlike the Irgun, which was absorbed into the Haganah the
moment independence was attained, the Stern Gang always
remained on the fringe of the regular army.

The Haganah was already a regular army, and, as the Nazi
defeat neared, it was preparing to change enemies but not to
give up the struggle. Its organization was entirely secret,
even though, from time to time, the British government
tolerated its existence. Already in the Haganah we find the
two characteristic traits of the future Israeli army: empiricism
and secrecy. In addition, it had already developed the arts of
circumventing blockades and the covert repair of all matériel, even when damaged and apparently unusable. Its
training, too, foreshadowed that of today. For the most part
nocturnal, it was characterized above all by long cross-
country marches: five-day strategic maneuvers. Inaugurated
before 1939, this policy of clandestine military training bore
fruit in 1945.

STRUGGLE AGAINST BRITAIN

With the world effectively at peace, the Anglo-Israeli conflict broke out again. Up until the end of 1945, however, the
Haganah had, despite the hostility of the British government,
collaborated with the occupation forces; after the assassination of Lord Moyne, it had gone so far as to turn over the
terrorists of the Stern Gang and the Irgun to the authorities,
or else it took the responsibility of preventing them from
doing harm by deporting them to collectivist colonies. The

stubborn refusal of the British to consider the Palestine question in a light favorable to the Jews put an end to this strange
collaboration. On December 30, 1945, David Ben-Gurion
published a declaration of the Jewish Agency, in which he
stated "that it was difficult to appeal to the Jewish community
to observe the law when the government of the Mandate
itself constantly violated the basic law of the country, as it is
set forth in the Palestine Mandate." It was, in fact, a declaration of war.

This war had a triple objective: to drive out the British, to
contain the Arabs, and to achieve recognition of Israel as a
free nation by all the peoples of the world. The battle developed on two levels: against the British and the Arabs
within the Palestinian frontiers and on the Mediterranean.
For, even more than arms, Israel needed soldiers. The Haganah's first task was to facilitate the immigration of the
thousands of displaced persons, survivors of concentration
camps who were waiting all over Europe to leave for the
promised land. Ever since the start of World War II old
tubs commanded by very young men had been trying to run
the British blockade, with mixed success: For one boat that
succeeded in delivering its human cargo, how many were
forced, on the orders of the British navy, to go to Cyprus or
the Island of Mauritius and to hand over their passengers,
who had survived Dachau or Auschwitz, to new jailers, who,
though they did not threaten their lives, were nonetheless
resolved to deprive them of their liberty? Some refugees
preferred to die, rather than to resume their endless pilgrimage. Such was the case of the crew and passengers of the
Struma and the *Patria,* who blew themselves up and sank
off the Palestinian coast before the horrified eyes of their coreligionists. Other ships, like the famous *Exodus,* were sent
from port to port all the way to Germany, their point of
departure—a hell that they could not leave.

Despite its repugnance, the Haganah itself, confronted
with a situation that grew worse from day to day, adopted

terrorism in its turn and aligned itself with the Irgun in acts of sabotage, sneak attacks, and assorted reprisals. The struggle became more and more savage. On October 31, 1945, a series of raids paralyzed all the railroads of Palestine as police patrol boats exploded in the harbors and bombs went off in the oil refineries of Haifa. Great Britain did not allow itself to be intimidated, and fifteen days later Mr. Bevin's government refused to admit to Palestine the 100,000 "displaced persons" who were vegetating in European camps. He agreed to the immigration of only 1,500 Jews a month, paying tribute on the same occasion to "the generosity of our Arab friends," who were kind enough to tolerate it.

A general strike and disturbances in the wake of this decision produced numerous victims all over Palestine: Nine Jews were killed and thirty-seven British soldiers wounded. The British government replied by sending 15,000 reinforcements. But they were not enough: The future state of Israel already had a strong army, its entire people, which the 85,000 British soldiers could not bring to its knees. The violence escalated: Executions, kidnapings, torture, deportations—the atrocities could no longer be reckoned. On one side, soldiers were hanged and their corpses exhibited publicly; on the other, young men were kidnaped and tortured to death as examples. Right up to the opening of debate on Palestine at Lake Success in October 1947, the Haganah was learning to wage subversive warfare against an enemy that was technologically superior and organized according to Western military traditions.

THE WAR OF INDEPENDENCE

On November 27, 1947, the General Assembly of the United Nations decided on partition of Palestine by a vote of thirty-three in favor, with thirteen abstentions. This decision represented the defeat of British policy in the Middle East. The two giants, the U.S.S.R. and the United States, both cast affirmative votes. The British had to give way. The Anglo-Jewish war was virtually over. Another began immediately. The Arab states formed a league to block U.N. policy. Its objective: extermination of the Jewish population. The Haganah had to learn a new form of combat.

Once again, the encounter between David and Goliath was repeated. On the side of David, the Jewish forces were estimated at 45,340 combatants (including, of course, women and children) armed with 10,073 rifles, 1,900 submachine guns, 672 two-inch mortars, 93 three-inch mortars, 500 cartridges for each rifle and 700 for each machine gun: no air force, no navy, no anti-aircraft or antitank weapons. On the side of Goliath, there was the whole Arab world, Islamic fanaticism represented by the armies of the different nations (Egypt, Syria, Jordan, Iraq, Lebanon, and so on): approximately 50,000 men armed with 150 heavy guns, 340 tanks, 176 planes, and 14 warships—and sustained by the active sympathy of the British Empire. But Goliath had a soft belly.

The partition of Palestine was scheduled for May 1948, and the war began with guerilla operations in December 1947. Arab bands infiltrated the territory in groups of 500 to 1,000 men. Their aim: to prevent the Jews from moving about the countryside, to halt convoys of weapons and provisions, to isolate and destroy Jewish merchants in areas where Arabs were in a majority. The British administration closed its eyes: Bands crossing the Jordan in broad daylight aroused no more than the curiosity of its officials.

Life quickly became intolerable; one could no longer leave the cities. Buses were regularly attacked and set afire. The passengers had to choose between facing bursts of submachine-gun fire and dying in the flames. It was no longer possible to go from Tel Aviv to Jerusalem. The critical point was reached in March 1948, when the Jews lost the battle of the roads, the group of villages of Kefar Etzion was taken by storm, a convoy was destroyed in Galilee, and two more were demolished on the road to Jerusalem. Arab indecision and internal rivalries saved Israel. Its luck changed on April 15, when convoys finally succeeded in reaching Tel Aviv, and the Jews shifted from the defensive to the offensive. Cities like Tiberias, Haifa, and Jaffa fell into the hands of the Israelis, who dug into their new stronghold. On April 24 the Arabs decided to salute the birth of the new state of Israel by flattening it with bombs.

From the very beginning of hostilities, Goliath had been winded. He had stalked the territories that were already virtually conquered, that is, wholly populated by Arabs, but he had stumbled on pebbles: the kibbutzim and the fortified villages defended by peasants armed with bottles of gasoline. The Jews managed, with Molotov cocktails, to destroy tanks that were in perfect condition. The Arab heavy artillery pounded away at farms that were hardly defended at all. The Arab air forces intervened with no result. The U.N., sympathetic to the Arabs, called for a cease-fire on June 11, but the Arabs saw in this pause an evil trick and took advantage of the truce to counterattack. This fury was to be fatal for them.

On July 9 the Israeli troops began an offensive. Everywhere, it was a rout. Lydda (the airport of Tel Aviv), Jerusalem, Nazareth, and then Galilee and the banks of the Jordan—all were retaken in ten days. It was a total collapse: The Arab leaders took to their heels first; the terrified people followed. The final reckoning was overwhelming: A little over 12 square miles of Jewish Palestine remained in the hands of the Arabs, but almost 500 square miles of Arab territory had passed into Jewish control. The Arabs' "show of force" had turned out to be catastrophic, and they therefore decided to return to guerilla tactics. Unfortunately, things had changed. Each raid was treated by the Jews as a provocation, which inevitably led to reprisals. The various Arab aggressions were followed by lightning raids that put all Israeli territory, then the Gaza Strip, and finally the Sinai desert under Jewish control.

On January 1, El 'Arish was invaded. Meanwhile, the Jewish forces, aided by the civilian population, which built up the country as the army conquered it, had obtained planes that were quite primitive but as effective against the up-to-date Arab plans as Molotov cocktails had been against Arab tanks. The Israeli victory became a triumph, whereupon there was an international reaction that foreshadowed many others: The United States and Great Britain called upon Ben-Gurion to halt his offensive and to evacuate the conquered territories. Ben-Gurion obeyed. The war continued, however, for a few more months. In January 1949, as if by accident, Israeli fighters shot down five British planes flying over their national territory. Britain did not protest. Two months later, on March 20, 1949, the war ended, and the Haganah could at last become the Israeli army.

This first war, which had lasted a year and a half, had left the Israelis with 6,000 dead, including 1,500 civilians. It was the toughest and most difficult of the Israeli wars. The Sinai campaign in 1956 would claim only 200 Israeli lives, all men under arms and half of them officers. It lasted ten days. The lightning war of 1967 would cause 820 deaths, all military, and would last six days.

THE NEW ISRAELI ARMY

In 1949, at the end of the war of independence, the Israeli army numbered 70,000 men, equipped with obsolete and ill-assorted matériel. The various units, born in the underground, differed in character and training. As a rule, they recognized only the commanders that they themselves had chosen. Yet the Jews had won, thanks to the determination of each combatant, who knew that his back was against the wall and that he could only conquer or die—and thanks also to Arab disorganization, lack of strategic planning, and internecine quarrels. Most of the Arabs had come to Palestine not to make war but to plunder, to rape, and to burn cities and villages, which they believed were defended only by a few weak militiamen. What was their surprise to find ranged before them an army risen from the earth, with weapons that had been hidden in the kibbutzim, uniforms manufactured in the cellars of Tel Aviv, and soldiers trained in the middle of the fields or in the shelter of orange groves between sessions of plowing or picking fruit!

Even so, several times in the course of the war of independence Israel narrowly escaped disaster. Although the Haganah displayed a great faculty for improvisation at all levels and individual men and women exhibited great courage, the training of recruits and the exercise of command left much to be desired. Officers did not keep the rosters of their men up to date. There was no supervision and very little discipline: Everyone followed his own instincts, even in the Palmach, the elite unit.

"I'm fed up with Dayan," Ben-Gurion once said (he had just learned that Dayan, the Chief of Staff, had personally participated in a reprisal raid on Jordan). "If he does it again I'll throw him in jail. He really believes that I can afford to lose a general!"

Nevertheless, during the Sinai campaign in 1956, the commanders of the big units continued to lead their men and to follow their instincts, which were, first of all, to push ahead. In his journal of the Sinai campaign, Moshe Dayan wrote:

Yesterday I had a stiff contretemps with the GOC Southern Command who, contrary to GHQ orders, sent the 7th Armoured Brigade into action before the appointed time. Despite the specific orders that armoured forces were not to be employed before the 31st, and explanations for this, the Southern Command considered that not a moment should be wasted and that immediately at the start of operations initiative as well as surprise should be exploited to advance and capture whatever one could. He accordingly resolved to send into action, on D-Day, all the forces at his command. As for the instructions of the General Staff and the military-political considerations that called for a different approach, the GOC Southern Command was not prepared to rely on the possibility that "someone else"—i.e. Anglo-French forces—might go into action and therefore saw no justification for holding up our main attack for forty-eight hours. He felt that GHQ orders on this matter were a political and military mistake for which we would pay dearly.

Dayan himself excused his subordinate:

As a matter of fact, for all my complaint both about the breach of discipline and the premature and poorly-planned action itself, I could not avoid a sympathetic feeling over the hastening of the brigade into combat even before they were required. Better to be engaged in restraining the noble stallion than in prodding the reluctant mule! (Moshe Dayan, *Diary of the Sinai Campaign,* New York: Schocken)

We shall encounter this noble stallion again. His name is General Ariel Sharon.

In July 1968 Colonel Reguev, commanding a brigade of paratroopers (the rank of colonel is the equivalent of a two-star general in France), personally led a few men in pursuit of a Palestinian commando group that had just crossed the Jordan. Reguev was thirty-five years old and considered one of the top Israeli specialists in counter-guerilla warfare; he was killed in hand-to-hand combat with the men of al-Fatah. The Israeli government protested and asked why it was absolutely necessary for its superior officers to expose themselves to fire as if they were privates. But Chief of Staff General Haim Barlev, successor to General Rabin (who had reached the age limit of forty-five), made it known that neither he nor the other general officers had any intention of abstaining thenceforward from putting themselves in the line of fire whenever they judged it necessary to do so.

Another problem during the war of independence was the attitude of the Haganah, born of the Hachomer, which did not manage to free itself from its original defensive orientation. It was still a rural militia. Its commanders had not stopped reminding the men under their command:

Your duty is to repel attacks, but don't let the smell of blood go to your heads. Remember that the name of our organization is "defense" and that our sole objective is to assure the security of our colonies. Our organization is at the service of this ideal; it is the instrument that allows us to live and work. It is the servant; it must never become the master.

In 1948 it was no longer enough to defend oneself; it was essential to attack, to conquer new lands before the Arabs seized them.

The arms workshops turned out weapons that, although they had the virtue of originality (as one can easily see from a visit to the Haganah museum in Tel Aviv), functioned for the most part very badly. A riddle of the time ran as follows: "What is the difference between a broom and a Sten gun [manufactured locally]?"

"There is a good chance that the broom will fire first."

The army had hardly emerged from underground when it had to confront two very serious crises. The first was a crisis of command that arose when Ben-Gurion sought to impose his authority directly on the army without going through all sorts of useless bodies that sometimes functioned at cross purposes, like the "national command," headed by Israel Galili, which duplicated the general staff, and the Security Committee, whose role no one understood very clearly. The Palmach was then subordinate to the pro-Soviet party, the MPAM (Labor Party). This minority party did not support the creation of a Jewish state, yet it controlled the only shock unit and, through Israel Galili, the supreme command of the Haganah and therefore of the armed forces.

Ben-Gurion wanted above all for the Haganah to become the army of the Jewish state and consequently to owe allegiance to no party, either of the extreme right or of the extreme left. The crises erupted on May 3, 1948, when Ben-Gurion fired Galili. On May 6 he received this letter, signed by all the commanders of the army:

The situation on the fronts at this moment necessitates the presence of a single authority at the head of the Haganah. The abolition of the post of chief of the national command and the illness of the chief of staff have left the Haganah without a qualified chief who has the authority to command brigades and to direct the general staff. This state of things has already disastrously harmed the conduct of the war during these last three days. The heads of the departments of the general staff consider the next few days decisive for the conduct of the war and the preparation for May 15. The heads of departments cannot continue to bear their heavy responsibilities so long as the matter is not settled. The heads of departments insist on the restoration of Israel Galili to his functions, pending final arrangements. If the matter is not settled in the next twelve hours, the heads of departments will cease to consider themselves responsible for the pursuit of the war. . . .

Ben-Gurion refused to yield, and it was the generals who submitted after obtaining a vague concession from the stubborn chief of a state that had not yet begun its existence. He agreed only to take Galili on as his deputy in charge of questions of mobilization, recruitment and regular soldiers.

"When I accepted this portfolio of defense," he told them, "it was with one aim in mind: to ensure the security of the country. In my role as chief of the armed forces I shall no longer recognize political parties."

On May 14 he proclaimed the Jewish state.

JEWISH CIVIL WAR

The second crisis was even more serious, for it caused Jewish soldiers to fire upon one another.

Early in the war, beside the Haganah—the illegal but official army of the Jewish Agency which numbered about 40,000 men, of whom only a few thousand were shock troops —there had existed a second army with about 3,000 resolute men: the Irgun. At the extreme of this already extremist movement were the "fighters for the freedom of Israel," better known as the Stern Gang, a few hundred very well-armed fanatical terrorists. Their prophet was Abraham Stern. As a student at Hebrew University in Jerusalem he had composed strange poems like one called "Psalms and Submachine Guns." After capture by the British in 1942, he was killed "while trying to escape." The struggle between the partisans of the Irgun and the Stern Gang, which constituted an extreme nationalist right, and those of the Haganah, who practiced *Havlagah* (moderation) and whose principles were socialist, began with counter-barrages of biblical quotations. The Haganah published anti-Irgun tracts inscribed with the Sixth Commandment: "Thou shalt not kill." The Irgun replied with a quotation from Exodus 21: 23–25: ". . . thou shalt give life for life, eye for eye, tooth for tooth, hand for hand, foot for foot, burning for burning, wound for wound, stripe for stripe."

From 1939 to 1942, terrorism resulted in only a few deaths: eight Jews, six Arabs, and eleven British policemen. In 1943 Menachem Beigin arrived in Palestine. He took the Irgun in hand and rallied to it all the elements of the Haganah who were exasperated by the Jewish Agency's policy of moderation. At the same time, about twenty Stern Gang leaders escaped from the concentration camp at 'Atrun.

In October 1944 Lord Moyne was assassinated in Cairo. Then the "hunting season" opened—the hunting season for men. It was a time in the history of Israel that no one likes to recall. Ben-Gurion decided to put an end to terrorism. On November 20, 1944, he ordered the Haganah to use all necessary means to stamp out the Irgun and the Stern Gang. Members of the dissident groups were to be eliminated from the independence movement. They were to be refused asylum when they were pursued, and when necessary Haganah members were to collaborate with the police and the British authorities to put the extremists away where they could do no harm.

Four hundred names of underground leaders were handed over to the British government by an emissary of the Jewish Agency. According to Arthur Koestler,

In addition, Haganah made a practice of warning the Government of terrorist actions in preparation. All this, however, did not suffice to stamp out terrorism; so the paradox was carried one step further when the illegal Haganah proceeded to enforce law and order by the illegal means of kidnapping and trapping their underground rivals. In December 1944 and January 1945, special Haganah detachments abducted from their homes a number of young men, who were mostly not directly connected with terrorism but members of the Revisionist Party, and suspected of being in the know about terrorist arms caches and hiding-places. The kidnapped men were put into Haganah "prisons"—that is, into a guarded house in one of the politically reliable collective settlements—and were interrograted by Haganah Intelligence men. The third-degree methods employed during these interrogations were in some cases on a par with those sporadically used by the Palestine C.I.D. Political Branch.

Though decimated, both the Irgun and the Stern Gang nevertheless continued to exist throughout this period. And the continuation of the White Paper policy, the blockade of the coast by vessels of the British fleet, and the offer of 1,500 immigration permits instead of the 100,000 that the Jewish Agency had asked for—all brought the Haganah and the extremists closer together for a time. On October 31, 1945, the Haganah itself embarked on a course of sabotage, blowing up bridges, railway switches, the Haifa oil refineries, and patrol boats of the maritime police. As everyone was indulging in terrorism, everyone fought side by side.

In one encounter, Haganah troops came up against a very solidly fortified Arab position. They blockaded it and took the necessary measures to capture it, subjecting themselves to the fewest possible losses in doing so. While the approaches were being prepared, some Stern Gang fanatics arrived on the scene. They were loaded down with explosives. They wanted to serve as living bombs and blow themselves up with the enemy fortifications. The Haganah soldiers prevented them from doing so by force, disarmed them, and, so to speak, defused them. Indignant, the boys of the Stern Gang staged a thirty-six-hour hunger strike.

Then came the war of independence, in which the Irgun collaborated with the Haganah. But the Irgun blew up the King David Hotel in Jerusalem, the seat of the British administration. Seventy-one people were killed, and the Jewish Agency protested:

The entire Yishuv [the Jewish community in Palestine] was shocked to the core by the criminal and abominable distortion which a dissident gang gave yesterday to the struggle of the Jewish people. This criminal massacre is senseless and inexcusable. . . . It is a crime committed not only against the dead and wounded, but against the Jewish community and its future.

There was a great deal of hypocrisy in this proclamation, for the Haganah had participated, at least indirectly, in the outrage. Then, to avenge a certain number of massacres perpetrated by the Arabs, like that on the colony of Kefar Etzion on April 9, 1948, Irgun soldiers attacked the Arab village of Bir Yassin and savagely massacred 254 men, women, and children.

Ben-Gurion protested, thundered, stormed, but "objectively" this butchery served the Jewish cause. Terrorism changed sides: The Arabs fell back, and the population abandoned entire provinces.

Finally on June 20, 1948, came the *Altalena* affair. Israel had just been proclaimed an independent state. After some difficult negotiations, the 3,000 men of the Irgun, constituting seven battalions, had been incorporated into the Haganah. It seemed, however, that these battalions, which remained an army within the army, had been issued equipment less complete than that of the other units. Beigin's aim as commander of the Irgun was to complete the arming of his men;

his emissaries therefore chartered the *Altalena,* a merchant ship of 5,500 tons, to transport an important cargo of arms and explosives (part of a gift of the French government) and 900 volunteers from Port-de-Bouc to Israel. Beigin intended to distribute 80 percent of this arsenal—including 5,000 rifles and 250 machine guns—to his battalions and to send only 20 percent on to Jerusalem. After interminable discussions, however, the Irgun decided to unload only its own weapons and reinforcements, without bothering about the government.

In general, arms purchases were made in total secrecy, but on this occasion the "secret" was a farce: "the ship was known to every secret agent, professional or amateur, in the Mediterranean basin" (Bar-Zohar, *Ben Gurion*).

The problem of the unity of the Israeli army and government—they were the same thing—was thus dramatically posed. ". . . the core of the conflict was a matter of prestige between two formerly rival underground groups, an extremist minority and a moderate majority, the latter of which had now attained the dignity of official Government and Army" (Koestler, *Promise and Fulfilment*). The affair was complicated by personal grudges, for the ship's commander, Dan Yamin, had, as a consequence of having been denounced by the Haganah during the "hunting season," spent several years in British prisons.

On June 20 the *Altalena* entered Israeli territorial waters and headed for the village of Kefar Vitkin, where hundreds of Irgun soldiers, who had deserted with their military vehicles, were waiting to transport the weapons. Ben-Gurion declared to the Council of Ministers:

The affair is of exceptional importance. There are not going to be two states and there are not going to be two armies. Beigin is not going to do as he pleases. I do not even wish to discuss at this time the political and international implications that would proceed from this violation of the truce; politics do not interest me in time of war. . . . But we must decide whether we are going to offer Beigin supreme authority or whether we are going to command him to stop his separatist activities. If he does not submit, we shall fire. . . .

During the night the 900 volunteers and some of the weapons were unloaded on the beach. But at dawn the Irgun soldiers were surrounded by government troops, armored cars, and artillery, while two corvettes, the first vessels of the Israeli navy, cut off the *Altalena's* retreat to the sea. At 4:00 P.M. the Haganah opened fire without notice; the members of the Irgun defended themselves as best they could, but they had to capitulate the following morning. There were forty dead. The ship set sail and reached Tel Aviv escorted by the two corvettes. There the captain ran his ship aground on the sand, where it served as a target for the entire government artillery in full view of the U.N. observers and foreign correspondents watching from the terraces of their hotels. Finally, the ship exploded. Beigin, the last man on board, had managed to get away. On the underground radio he accused Ben-Gurion of being a coward, an imbecile, and a dictator. But the Irgun had ceased to exist as an armed movement. The Israeli army had just sealed its unity in blood and at the risk of civil war. That unity was never again put in question. The battalions of the Irgun were dissolved and their men assigned to other units.

We shall not recapitulate the various struggles that pitted the Haganah, first against terrorist gangs and against the regular armies of the Arab countries in 1948–1949. It was the longest and hardest war in the history of Israel. Numerous errors were committed by the Jews, but they were compensated for by tenacity and courage. The Arabs made still more mistakes, and fought in defiance of common sense, without tactics, throwing themselves in waves against entrenched positions and fleeing as soon as the Jews struck back. The Egyptian army thought only of seizing the territories that might revert to Jordan, forgetting, in its complacency, the existence of a Jewish army that, though dressed in rags and carrying old rifles, would cut it to pieces.

In the Israeli army of 1968 we still find many traditions inherited from the clandestine Haganah and even from the Irgun. It is still an army that marches on foot, though thoroughly motorized, and that insists, as it always has, on the need to know the terrain perfectly, down to its tiniest corners and its narrowest pathways, by night as well as by day. The pilots march as much as the paratroopers do, and they are trained as paratroopers before they learn to fly. The tank men also march, and they are prepared to fight as foot soldiers when they lose their tanks. The girls march as much as the men, and so do the schoolchildren of the Gadna, who, at the age of fourteen, already carry rifles on their backs. All ranks continue to address one another familiarly and to use first names, as during the war of liberation; the soldiers get to know one another intimately, and will risk their lives to save a wounded comrade. In July 1948 forty men were killed under the walls of the fortress of Nebi Yusha in the act of bringing back the body of their fallen commander. Similar incidents occurred in the course of the Six-Day War. The Israeli army never leaves its corpses behind. As in the Haganah, officers and soldiers still wear the same uniform and eat the same food in the same mess halls. The commander continues to march ahead of his men, regardless of all the rules and customs that prevail in other armies.

COUP D'ÉTAT BY THE MILITARY

The most recent crisis in the army occurred just before the outbreak of the Six-Day War in May 1967. On this subject, Deputy Chief of Staff General Ezer Weizmann, serving under General Rabin, said, "I don't believe that a coup d'état could have occurred, but we have never been so close to it."

At the end of May the entire country went through a frightful week. An atmosphere of catastrophe and despair had been created by the hesitations of the Israeli government, which vacillated between war and peace, and also by Foreign Minister Abba Eban's falsely optimistic interpretations of his interviews with Lyndon Johnson, Charles de Gaulle, and Harold Wilson—interpretations that were contradicted by other information. It is also necessary to mention a stammering radio speech by President Levi Eshkol, his maneuvers to prevent Moshe Dayan from replacing him at the Defense Ministry, and the exasperation of the mobilized troops and officers, whose only distraction was to listen to the calls for murder being broadcast on the Arab radio stations.

General Rabin was the victim of a nervous collapse. General Weizmann, who temporarily replaced him (after threatening to throw his stripes in his face), told Eshkol: "Awaiting your commands is the strongest army since the kingdom of David. Give the army the order to march, and you will become the great victor of the war of Israel. If you don't, you will be responsible for the destruction of the country. Your policy is leading straight to the annihilation of the third Jewish state."

General Ariel Sharon, the father of the paratroopers, told Eshkol, "Your shilly-shallying is going to cost us thousands of lives."

Finally the civil power yielded. Moshe Dayan, who is little loved in peacetime because of his cynicism, his undisguised ambition, and his nonconformity, took over the Ministry of Defense. Everyone, from Nasser to de Gaulle, understood that giving such a post to such a man meant war. It was also a break with a tradition established by Ben-Gurion, that the Prime Minister is Minister of Defense as well.

What would have happened if the Eshkol government had not put an end to its temporizing? A military coup d'état? Today, this possibility is denied. But between May 20 and June 1, the date when Moshe Dayan became Minister of Defense, "promoted by the 80,000 Egyptians who had entered the Sinai," such a coup d'état was considered possible and even hoped for. Victory has made people forget those dark days, but many people still think about what General Rabin said: "In this country, the only force that can be counted on is the army."

Happily, that army is not isolated from the nation; it encompasses the whole nation and can act only with its total approval. Then where is the coup d'état?

A GENERAL VIEW OF THE TSAHAL

Before pursuing our study of this army—born of the night and delighting in mystery—we shall try to sketch a broad outline of its organization, which is not an easy thing to get to know, for everything in Israel is a military secret.

Arthur Koestler wrote (this happened in June 1948):

Our escort was a young man of German-Jewish origin called Shlomo (Hebrew for Solomon). His surname we never found out, nor that of any of the officers and local commanders with whom we talked and travelled along the fronts. It was all part of the atmosphere of dark secrecy in which the Haganah shrouded itself. These men had so long lived underground that the habit of conspiracy had become second nature to them, and now they could not get out of it. The unique practice of keeping even the names of the General Staff and Army Commanders secret had already produced a swarm of pernicious rumours in the foreign Press to the effect that the Jewish Army was run by Soviet generals on active service. At the first Press conference we attended in Tel Aviv the public information officer introduced a young man as the General Officer Commanding Operations without mentioning his name. An American journalist had a crack at him with "How do you spell your name, sir?" but was told that for "security reasons" the G.O.C.'s identity could not be disclosed.

Nothing has changed since then.

The Israeli army that won the Six-Day War is composed of regular units, reserves, and a territorial-defense force. First of all, there is a nucleus of career officers and warrant officers. The latter, the "master sergeants," are a legacy from the British army; they handle training and instruction of young officers and warrant officers, the maintenance of equipment, supply depots, and administration. These regular units are very small and not very well paid. A lieutenant receives 800 Israeli pounds a year, of which 30 pounds are withheld for taxes. Active service currently lasts three years for men from eighteen to twenty-one years old and twenty months for women from eighteen to twenty years old. The active army, with its permanent units and its recruits combined, hardly exceeds 40,000 men.

Second, there is an army of reserves, who are subject to very intense training, generally for one month each year. In 1968, because of the occupation of conquered territories and the resurgence of terrorism, some stayed up to three months in the services. The reserves form the basis of the Israeli defense corps and can be mobilized at any moment and with surprising speed. Often, between the time a reserve paratrooper leaves his job and the time he arrives at the front lines less than forty-eight hours elapse—twenty hours for the first reserve. "What is a reservist in Israel?" I asked an artillery commander who had just been recalled with this unit to the frontier.

"Well, monsieur, a reservist is an active soldier who is allowed, for ten or eleven months a year, to earn a living for himself and his family in the civilian sector."

The reserve army consists of approximately 260,000 men.

Finally, there is a territorial-defense organization based on the fortified kibbutzim on the frontier and in the interior and on the units of soldier-colonists in the Nahal.

The army is organized in the following services:

• a tactical air force equipped mainly with fighters and fighter-bombers. There are no heavy bombers. The service's primary mission is to destroy the enemy air force in order to gain air supremacy and then to support the tanks and ground forces. The same aircraft are used for both purposes.

- a mechanized armored corps.
- mobile weapons outfits divided into brigades of about 3,000 men each. A brigade possesses its own support weapons and independent quartermaster service.
- general reserve units: artillery, engineers, paratroopers, or commandos.
- territorial-defense groups, a sort of national guard composed of veterans.
- a navy charged with protecting the coasts and composed of a few patrol boats, several minesweepers, and some submarines. At the outbreak of war in 1967 this navy was six times smaller than that of Egypt. The Israelis have always neglected their navy in favor of other armed services.

During the Six-Day War, even by scraping the bottom of every barrel, the Israelis were never able to mobilize more than 300,000 men. (This official figure was given to me by General Tsur, Moshe Dayan's deputy and the Minister of Defense.)

The Intelligence Services

According to the experts, Israel's most effective service is neither its air force, its tank corps, nor its paratroopers, but its intelligence service, and we shall therefore talk about this service first. Officially, it is composed of five sections:

• the "Mossad," the equivalent of the French S.D.E.C.E. [or the American C.I.A.], whose agents operate abroad and which reports directly to the President of the Council. It has an information-gathering branch and an action branch. It was the latter that kidnaped Adolf Eichmann and tracked down the German scientists working for Nasser. The celebrated Israeli spy Elie Cohen belonged to it.

• the "Modiin," similar to the French *deuxième bureau* [or the British M.I.5], which is exclusively occupied with military intelligence.

• the department of research and documents attached to the Ministry of Foreign Affairs, which is responsible, in particular, for studying the political situation in the neighboring Arab countries.

• the Shin Beth, internal-security and counterespionage service.

• the bureau of investigation parallel to the French D.S.T. [Direction de la Surveillance du Territoire] and to the Shin Beth, of which it is the executive organ. It is in charge of surveillance and arrests. This whole service is directed by an "appointed official of the security services of the state," who is subject to the control of a restricted committee of the Israeli parliament ever since Israel Harel's tenure, during which he caused all sorts of catastrophes, including Ben-Gurion's departure from the government.

Harel was a most unusual person, who personally took part in such operations as the kidnaping of Eichmann in Buenos Aires. He himself visited his agents in the Arab countries. In 1963 he discovered that Ben-Gurion's military counselor, Colonel Israel Beer, was a Soviet agent. He did not know enough to keep his revelations secret, and the vindictive Ben-Gurion avenged himself over the affair of the German scientists who supposedly had developed the "absolute weapon" for Nasser. Harel had sent them parcels containing explosives and had even supervised the kidnaping of the daughter of one of them. But Harel had allowed himself to be fooled by spies endowed with too-vivid imaginations. The "absolute weapon" turned out to be only a bad missile whose guidance mechanism was inadequate.

Ben-Gurion, who had no intention of compromising his excellent relations with West Germany, which was paying very heavy reparations to Israel in the form of subsidies and weapons, ordered Harel to stop fooling around. Mad with rage, Harel resigned and was replaced by another chief, whose name, of course, was kept secret. The current incumbent is General Amit, about whom very little is known.

Officially, General Yariv heads only three of the five sections of the Israeli secret services, that is, only those that are related to the army. But it is certain that he plays at least a leading role in all the Israeli secret services.

YARIV SPEAKS

General Yariv is the oldest of all the Israeli generals. He is forty-seven, and only the very special character of his activities has permitted this violation, not of the regulations—

the Israeli army has none, just as the country has no formal
constitution—but of the customs that prevail. Yariv was born
in a kibbutz and first studied in an agricultural school. From
1941 to 1946 he served in the British army; then he was sent
to a school founded by the Jewish Agency, where he was
trained as a diplomat. The war made him a soldier.

In 1950, at twenty-nine, he looked twenty-four and was a
colonel. He was sent to study at the War College in Paris.
The commandant of the school took him aside and said to
him: "My friend, you really look too young for your rank.
This could upset the other students. Please, come to class in
civvies."

Since 1964 Yariv has been at the head of the military intelligence services. Every morning at 6:00 he leaves his house
alone to take the wheel of his American car, which sprouts
radio antennas in profusion, and drives slowly off. He lives in
a residential district of Tel Aviv, and all his neighbors say,
with a knowing air, "There's our master spy going to work."
Everybody knows everybody in the little village that is Israel.
It is also impossible to disguise losses, as the Arabs have
learned so well. Yariv is an affable and discreet man, endowed with a prodigious memory. The American writer
Barbara Tuchman says of him:

He is capable of spending an hour with 150 journalists from all
over the world, of captivating them without telling them a thing,
of answering questions with the agility and skill at feinting of a
fencing champion, but of doing all this with so much charm that
in the end 150 journalists applaud enthusiastically, convinced that
they have just truly learned all the secrets of Israel. . . . There is
in him a curious mixture of the clear and simple logic of a teacher
and the intuition of an actor.

The day after the victory in the Six-Day War, Moshe
Dayan, when asked about the role played by intelligence,
could only answer, "All I can say is, the role of intelligence
was just as important as that of the aircraft and the tanks."

It was Yariv and his services that decided the hour of the

surprise air attack on the Egyptian bases: 7:45 A.M., Monday, June 5 (8:45 A.M. Egyptian time). Yariv had learned from his spies that the Egyptian air force, on permanent alert since May 16, relaxed its vigilance for one hour (from 8:45 to 9:45) when the pilots went off to eat breakfast. When the Israeli air force attacked, the Egyptian pilots were all at the table eating buttered toast and drinking coffee.

On the morning of June 5 the Israeli radio directed a number of appeals in Arabic to the Egyptian pilots. The speaker addressed them directly, calling them by their names, including their first names, and even invoking the names of their wives and children. He advised them not to bomb Tel Aviv but to drop their bombs into the sea.

The editor in chief of the Egyptian newspaper *al-Ahram*, Monsieur Heykal, a close friend of Nasser, wrote in July 1968: "The Israelis had a perfect knowledge of Egypt. They even knew the names of our pilots, as well as the secret codes of our air force and our tank corps."

Sometimes sheer chance makes it possible to lift a corner of the veil covering the mysterious activities of the "master spy." While the tanks of General Israel Tal were pushing toward the canal from the Sinai, they picked up radio messages addressed to them by an Egyptian officer. These messages gave the exact placements of the enemy artillery and the movements of the enemy tanks, which were regrouping to cut off the Israelis' route. This invaluable information enabled the Israelis to annihilate the enemy very quickly. But the Egyptian officer who had provided the intelligence was killed during the battle. He was shot down by a patrol of his own countrymen while trying to reach the Israeli lines, for this "Egyptian" was one of Yariv's Israeli agents. The order was given to bring him back to Israel and to bury him there. His name is still unknown.

General Yariv is a small man with gray hair and alert, piercing eyes. In truth, he does sometimes resemble a professor in his compulsion to explain himself clearly and at length, but this trait is only one aspect of an extremely complex personality. Like all "master spies," he has neither personal sympathies nor personal antipathies. Feelings, virtues, vices are simply means to be used toward a single end: the defense of Israel. He granted me an interview—he talks readily to journalists—not out of vain desire for publicity but in order to provide me with enough information so that I wouldn't look for it elsewhere. He also wished me to forget the atmosphere of secrecy and defiance that is often so distressing in Israel and that can occasionally lead one to imagine himself in a people's republic.

General Yariv speaks excellent French. Whenever I look as if I don't understand, he repeats his sentences but evades with consummate skill all questions that seem awkward to him.

"Our intelligence services," he tells me, "and kindly be good enough to believe me, are not as extraordinary as people are always saying."

I protest, and this protest clearly does not displease him. He continues: "But if they seem so effective to you, it is because our combat units all recognize the importance of detailed intelligence. They also know how to use the information that we furnish them. The first duty of an intelligence chief, in my opinion, is to furnish fighting units—in time— with the information they need to fight effectively and to push forward. It is very easy to lose sight of this absolute imperative. Intelligence has no value in itself; it is not a product for the private consumption of insiders. It must above all be useful to the greatest possible number as quickly as possible. To procure operational intelligence we use the orthodox methods current in all other armies. There is, however, one difference. Our military men have always been accustomed to waging war by putting to use the information at their disposal. They have never forgotten, either, that they must transmit as much of it as possible to us. There is a continuous current flowing between us and all the active units. Information comes in from a given point and is instantly circulated throughout the army. This cult of intelligence in our army has roots in our clandestine past. In the Palmach— I belonged to the Palmach—intelligence techniques were already well developed. For example, we had to prepare very thick dossiers on all the Arab villages in the vicinity of our agricultural colonies. We had to know not only the buildings in those villages but also the families, relations among them and among different clans, the rivalries, the names of men who were likely to fight each other, and so on.

"Alongside what was already a documentation service, and always in perfect liaison with it, were our groups of scouts. Through perpetual patrols by day and night, especially by night, they learned to know the enemy, his positions, his defenses, and his opportunities for maneuver; above all they acquired a perfect knowledge of the terrain on which, sooner or later, they might have to fight. The slightest alteration in topography was instantly noted, for example the construction of a wall of a new house. If we won in 1948, it was because of our excellent knowledge of the terrain. If we won again in 1956 and 1967, it was for the same reason. Never forget that our battlefields are always the same ones.

"There is nothing exceptional in our orthodox intelligence gathering. Like everybody else, we use aerial photography and geographical and geological maps. We send out patrols to find out what the enemy is up to. We infiltrate agents who transmit information to us by radio and also take photographs. But at any moment we must be ready to make war. Therefore our operational intelligence work has to be continuous. Thus for the southern military region, the Sinai, we never ceased to update our intelligence as new information came to us from different sources, for we knew that this region would perforce become a battleground again. We were one of the first armies in the world, if not the first, to use maps and aerial photos on such a large scale, to distribute

them even among the minor units. We are the least miserly people imaginable with intelligence information. We place full reliance on the lowest echelons of command. Most of our soldiers are reserves, as are the majority of the intelligence officers who accompany our troops.

"Has the reservist a greater alertness, a greater curiosity than the regular? We have never had occasion to do other than congratulate ourselves on our intelligence officers. Of course, we keep them posted, we make them take courses of instruction, we teach them everything we know, for we are sure of their discretion—why yes, because of that very taste for secrecy, sometimes carried to the point of mania, of which you so often complain and that is for us a strength. We need secrecy to survive, and we need men who know how to keep their mouths shut and listen to others.

"That is one aspect of my services. That is not the only one. Our greatest preoccupation is to do everything possible to be able to predict for the army and the government when war will break out and to do so in time to mobilize our forces: This interval must never exceed four days. Of course, operational intelligence then becomes political. Look at a map of Israel, at least as it was before our conquests in the Six-Day War. In the plain of Sharon behind Netanya our territory was no more than ten miles wide, about eleven miles to the north and sixteen miles below. The Jerusalem corridor at its widest point measured eleven miles. We had 50 miles of common frontiers with Lebanon, 48 with Syria, 330 with Jordan, and 145 with Egypt. This particular strategic situation, and the little time available to us to find our feet in case of a surprise attack, did not permit us to make mistakes. To make mistakes became a crime.

"Let's look for a moment at our situation: 70 million Arabs against 2.2 million Jews. These Arabs, it's true, are not yet capable of uniting. But in certain circumstances they can get together within the framework of common action. That was the case in May 1967, when one saw an Egyptian general,

for example, giving orders in Amman to King Hussein's Arab Legion. Although we hardly fear a united Arab front, we can always come up against a unified command."

I ask, *"Won't the Russians manage to bring about this unification of the Arabs and to succeed where the British failed?"*

"That would be a marriage between the cart and the horse, so different are the Arab countries from one another. What common ground, at least as far as political systems are concerned, can exist among Nasserite Egypt, Saudi Arabia, Baathist Syria, and Jordan, with its little king defended by Bedouin and Circassians?

"No, the Russians don't want, for the moment, to push pan-Arabism systematically. They are seeking only to bring about the unification of the so-called "progressive" Arab countries: Egypt, Syria, Iraq. But it's like Penelope's task, for the cloth unravels as quickly as it is woven.

"In truth, the Arabs' greatest weakness arises from a human factor, the gap between the desire to do something and the inability to carry it through with which they are afflicted. It is difficult for a Western person to feel at ease with two or more contradictory truths struggling inside him. The Arab accommodates himself to this without difficulty. From that comes his weakness and his lack of logic, tenacity, and faith. There is no cause that he does not whole-heartedly embrace and that he cannot betray with the same good faith, without ceasing to believe in it. There are the innumerable examples of all those Arab leaders who preach socialism with all sincerity and continue at the same time to lead the lives of capitalists, or even of feudal overlords, without the slightest embarrassment.

"I remember interviewing an Egyptian general whom we captured last year in the Sinai. I was interested in the Egyptian army's training methods. For two hours he explained to me in detail how recruits were trained, how officers were educated, how exercises were combined with maneuvers.

*Everything seemed to me logical, perfect, well conceived:
There was nothing to be said against it. Suddenly, my Egyp-
tian general interrupted himself and shrugged his shoulders:
'But mostly we just painted over.'*

"Astonished, I questioned him further: 'What do you mean,
painted over?'

" 'You know how one slaps a coat of paint on rusty old
ships to make people think they're new. It's easier than patch-
ing them up, and besides it produces a better effect. Instead
of training, we inundated our general staff with reports on
the carrying out of exercises and the progress of training. But
in reality we didn't do the work; it was nothing but a paint
job.'

"The fellow intrigued me; I asked him, 'But you knew
that you were going to fight a war sooner or later?'

" 'Yes, but war is different.'

"I couldn't for the life of me get it through his head that
war and training are indissolubly linked.

"This Arab ambivalence! Take another example: I ran
into one of our Arab agents who works for us in Syria. At last,
a spy, eh? We talked shop. I wanted, however, to know more
about him; it's one of my principles to know the men I employ thoroughly. This one worked for [he rubbed his thumb
and index finger together] money; it's most often the case. I
asked him, 'What do you think of Nasser?'

"Without hesitation he answered, 'I admire Nasser greatly;
I would follow him anywhere.'

" 'Why?'

" 'Because he is one of the rare authentic Arab nationalists,
and I am, like him, a true Arab nationalist!'

" 'But you work for us, who are Jews, and therefore your
enemies and those of Nasser.'

" 'Oh, that's different. That's work!'

"In these Arab countries, the word assumes prime importance. East Asia, the Asia of China, is the land of the sign,
India, that of the gesture, the Middle East and Arab Africa

that of the word. Thanks to the word, victories become defeats and defeats victories, for the word means more than the reality and is enough to change it. It is for this reason that most of the reports of officers to their colonels, of colonels to their generals, and of generals to Nasser are false and full of lies. Isn't the word more real than what exists? Change the word and the reality will change! In all this is blended the confusion and the lack of logic born of this civilization of the word. Thus, Arab propaganda presents the Israelis, at one and the same time, as cowards, terrified little hunched Jews who tremble before the Egyptian colossus, and as Zionist bandits with butcher knives in our teeth and terrifying faces, diabolical creatures endowed with supernatural powers. These contradictions don't bother anybody.

"In a quiet period, in time of peace, the Arabs paint over, and everything is more or less fine. But when war suddenly breaks out, then the word gives way to the fact, the dream to harsh reality. Lying is no longer possible, and everything collapses. The Arab armies turn out to be incapable of improvising the slightest maneuver or even of correctly executing a classic movement. The men are not trained to march on foot or to use their tanks. No training, nothing but painting over. The paint cracks open, and the rust shows through. The officers, instead of giving their men an example of courage, give them a bad example by taking to their heels. Of course, there are exceptions. It is interesting to note that the Arab armies that fight best are the least politicized. This was so, in particular, with King Hussein's Arab Legion, which had no political tradition at all but only a military tradition. It fought better than the Egyptians and the Syrians—especially the Syrians, who were politicized to an extreme. The Arabs' great tragedy in military matters is their inability to improvise, their hopeless inability to take any initiative whatever in tactical or strategic matters. Is this because of the very heavy weight of their history? Their military thought is, after all, doctrinaire and dogmatic. The Russians, who have just taken

them in hand, can only push them still farther in this direction, for they themselves are doctrinaire and dogmatic. I also think the Arabs fight badly because the overwhelming majority of them do not feel that our presence in the Middle East constitutes a mortal danger. This is so true that the Arab countries have been able to lose three wars in a row and continue to exist. Nasser is still in power. For us Jews, to win is above all to survive; one lost battle can mean the end of us."

I returned to this problem of the Russians, which so greatly preoccupies the Israelis: "Doesn't the presence of the Russians in the Middle East threaten to make your job of gathering intelligence more difficult, for you will now find adversaries of your own caliber in this area? Aren't the Russians going to find agents in Israel who will act this time for ideological reasons rather than for money—Jews for whom being a Communist is even more important than being a Jew? You surely have a Communist Party here?"

General Yariv makes a gesture of denial with his finger.

"It's true, we have a Communist Party in Israel, but I hardly see those Communists working against us. Fortunately, there was Stalin in Russia, with his anti-Semitism. We really ought to erect a statue to him for that. It is certain that the Russians are going to improve the Arabs' intelligence methods, but not to the point of making them really dangerous. The best agents that the Russians send into Israel, directly or by way of the Arabs, are most often Armenians. They are men who have a taste for adventure and also for money. They speak many languages and can be quite effective. This was true of Yakobian, whom we seized as the result of an inexcusable error. He passed for a Jew, but on his passport it said, born in Salonika (Turkey). In truth, I have never known a single Arab agent who was really first-class, a single one who could be compared to Elie Cohen. Arab agents are often caught because of the indiscretions of their chiefs. When one of their men pulls something off, a brilliant feat, or boasts

about having done so, his commanding officer cannot long resist the pleasure of boasting about it to the people around him. All it takes is one pair of ears in his entourage for us to be informed. Betrayed by its chief in Cairo or Damascus, the rat is simply caught in its trap in Jerusalem, Tel Aviv, or Beersheba."

"How does the future of Israel look to you?"

"I don't believe that an entente is possible at this moment between the Israelis and the Arabs. Our relations are not governed by any logic; they are emotional in character, at least on the Arab side. 'Time is on our side,' the Arabs say, 'and one day the Arab ocean will again cover up the little Jewish island.' It's what has already happened with the Crusaders. It's true that the Arabs have time. But we are in a hurry, and we act quickly. As long as the problem of the Palestinian refugees exists, it will be difficult for an Arab leader to make peace. He would immediately be executed for treason. Nasser said a few years ago that he would gladly meet Ben-Gurion but that he would not survive that meeting by as much as four hours. At the same time, these Arab leaders couldn't care less about the Palestinian refugees. No, the solution to our problems must be found in Jordan, in making that country a kind of Palestinian buffer between ourselves and the Arabs."

"Every moment of your life, every moment of your day, you must be thinking about war. Aren't you tired?"

"It is exhausting, and it is for this reason that generals are not allowed to grow old in their posts. But living in Israel is so great a compensation for me that I accept all the risks and all the burdens. And then our situation is far from being desperate. We must extract maximum strategic advantage from our victory. Political pressures may well be exerted to force us to hand back the territories we are occupying. But we can count on the Arabs: They will help us. They aren't going to change their attitude and behavior all that quickly. They will continue to be disunited, and their history will

continue for a long time to be that perpetual succession of revolutions, coups d'état, revenges, assassinations, and treason. One day they will tire of the Russians; everybody tires of the Russians sooner or later. Of course, we are in a difficult situation. Of the 2.2 million inhabitants that Israel now contains, 270,000 are Arabs. With the occupied territories this Arab population increases by 1,120,000. Then the problem of subversion arises. I think that we're going to have trouble in this area, serious trouble."

I leave General Yariv to his secrets. He has not revealed much to me, and that is as usual. He is going to continue to wage his secret war in countries and on battlefields about which he cannot and does not want to talk to me. Today he would gladly fight the entire world so that Israel might survive. Tomorrow, perhaps, I shall encounter him again, this time without his uniform, as the director of a firm or a university professor, still just as eloquent and still just as discreet. Today it is necessary to eliminate al-Fatah. This border struggle is not a classic type of guerilla warfare. The Arab populations don't like the Israelis. They are more sympathetic to al-Fatah but not to the point of cooperating with it—which is, perhaps, good luck for Israel.

THE KURDS AND THE DRUSES

The various Israeli secret services play, on the periphery of the Arab world and among the minorities that exist within this Arab world, a determined, dangerous, and effective game. It is no longer a secret to anyone that the Kurds are aided by the Israelis. They receive not only weapons and matériel but also instructors. Two western journalists claim that a certain number of paratroop officers of the Tsahal live in the entourage of the old Mullah Mustafa Barzani. It must have been they who established his communications network and trained his commandos in sabotage and demolition. I recall with amusement the time in 1946 that I met Barzani in northern Iran. He was then a protégé of the U.S.S.R. and even wore the uniform of a Soviet general.

The Iranians have little love for the Arabs, who once pushed tactlessness to the point of trying to rename the Persian Gulf the Arabian Gulf. The Kurds have now been Iranian by nationality and language for about ten years; as they are no longer supported by the Soviets, who dropped them to espouse the Arab cause, the Iranian government, army, and special services have treated them with great understanding. The Israelis, on the other hand, enjoy excellent relations with Persia. In this matter of the Kurds, Persia and Israel pursue common ends: to prevent the reconstitution of a dangerous Arab empire called "socialist" to disguise its pan-Islamism. If Iran were to become a rear base for Barzani's Kurds and also a forward base of some value to Israel, I would not be unduly surprised.

There are plenty of other minorities in the Arab world that are, if not as active, at least as discontented as the Kurds, especially the Druses. A certain number of Druses are already serving in the Israeli army and in the frontier guard. They have always shown themselves loyal to the State of Israel since its foundation in 1948. Numerous Druses also live in Syria and Lebanon. When the Israelis took the Golan Heights, the entire Syrian population, whether Christian or Moslem, fled toward Damascus. El Quneitra, a town that had formerly had 11,000 inhabitants, was entirely deserted. Not a cat or a dog remained, and smashed furniture rotted on the sidewalks. Through the roofs of churches and mosques one could see daylight. But in contrast the Druses, who had remained in their villages, seemed to get along very well with the Israeli troops. This relationship didn't smack of collaboration but rather of friendship. The Israelis were full of attentions to them. They respected their customs and their peacefulness. They even gave them food and seeds. The military police came to chase me out of one of their villages on the pretext that I was bothering these people.

Thanks to this police clumsiness, I realized that the Druse problem is taboo. Israel is hoping to win over this considerable minority but does not want it known. It probably has the same intention with respect to other Christian minorities, although in occupied Jordan, at least, the Christian Arabs are for the moment as hostile to the Israelis as are the Moslems. Perhaps they have no desire to look like collaborators, and as the notion of collaboration is very loosely defined in these fanatical countries, they are wary. After the battle of Sinai, the Egyptians who reoccupied the Gaza Strip shot everyone accused of collaborating with the Jews, even the ordinary policemen, who, though disarmed by the Israelis, had continued to direct traffic in the streets of Gaza. Weak and frightened people often perpetrate such cruelties.

Despite appearances, the Israelis are not really encircled by Arabs, or at least this encirclement is a sieve. The internal struggle in Syria and Iraq between different factions of the Baath; the "financial realism" of the Lebanese; the indifference of the Egyptian population toward Nasser, his colonels, and his generals, who know only how to lose wars and ride around in Mercedes; the fratricidal wars in Yemen; the apathy of a whole class of intellectuals and small collective landowners—all these factors enable Israeli agents to pursue an extremely effective and profitable political course. One day I asked an Israeli general who was telling me about the mistakes made by Nasser and his army "if *le Raïs* wasn't an Israeli secret agent named Moshe or Ygal."

"He deserves to be," he answered with a laugh.

"How many political parties are there in Syria?" I was asked one day by the tank colonel whose units were occupying the Syrian town of El Quneitra and the surrounding area. I confessed my ignorance.

"Well, there are three: the first army corps, the second army corps, and the third army corps. When we attacked the Golan Heights, defended by the second army corps, after our first breakthrough, all the troops of that army corps ran away. More than defeat the officers feared that the first army corps would take power and grab their jobs. We followed them to within about ten miles of Damascus. Then we were stopped and finally pulled back because our government was afraid of Soviet intervention."

"And if you had to take Damascus today?"

The answer could not have been more laconic: "No problem on the military level: three brigades, seven hours. But impossible on the political level. The Russians are there."

Through a window, he pointed to the building he was living in, a small bump on the landscape. "It is those who are supervising the constructions of the new fortifications who will have to defend Damascus. We hear them talk on the radio. We also know that certain Syrian officers are beginning to get fed up with Soviet tutelage. The Arabs say, 'We have time; the Jews will leave one day.' They're wrong. It's we who have time. We won't have to wait very long to see them at each other's throats again, dumping their current protectors, as they dumped the Egyptians in the past."

The Arabs themselves recognize the defects of their intelligence services. An analysis of these deficiencies like the one made by Edouard Saab (*La Syrie, ou la revolution dans la rancoeur,* Paris: Julliard) frequently confirms what General Yariv told me. He writes:

From that lightning war which in less than six days dismantled three Arab armies, one can extrapolate some constant elements that are from this time on established.

First, the chronic deficiency of the Egyptian intelligence services and those of the Arabs in general. It is now established that President Nasser was always very badly informed about the capacities and intentions of his enemies. As much in his conflicts with the other Arab countries that refused to submit to his leadership (Syria, Jordan, Tunisia, Yemen) as in the two wars he has fought with Israel, in 1956 and 1967, he was constantly mistaken in his estimates and frequently plunged into dead-end courses. As for the illusions of the masses and the dreams that they believed themselves entitled to entertain, they were owing to empirical considerations favored by the numerical disproportion of the forces on the scene, by the alleged prodigious promises of the U.S.S.R., and by the considerable quantity of weapons and munitions supplied by the Soviet Union.

Second, the extremely effective talent of the Israeli espionage services, abreast of all the Arab military secrets and of their strategic plans. It is true that they were assisted by the American C.I.A., but the presence in every Arab state of double agents—like the celebrated Elie Cohen, who under a false name and with a Syrian passport availed himself of his status as an emigrant to Argentina to "reenter" Syria and was able, in a few months, to win the blind trust of the Baath, to the point of participating in the deliberations of its executive committee—was to contribute notably to facilitating the Israelis' task. During the very first hours after the opening of hostilities, all the Syrian strategic points—landing strips, underground airfields, munitions dumps—were spotted, bombed, and put out of action. The presence of the Soviets in the Middle East seriously threatens to complicate the task of the Israeli intelligence services. It was they, apparently, who discovered the Israeli agent Elie Cohen and handed him over to the Syrians.

Cohen was hanged on May 18, 1965 in Damascus, after having lived for years in the very bosom of the dominant Syrian party, the Baath, as the friend of officers of the Syrian secret service whose material existence and feminine liaisons he helped along and from whom he extracted priceless information. He even offered a mink coat to the wife of the President of the Syrian Republic and a check for $10,000 to the Baath, which probably ended up in the President's pocket. On his corpse, sewn up in a white sack, the sentence of the military tribunal was inscribed in black letters: "Eliahou Ben Shaul Cohen was condemned to death in the name of the Arab people of Syria, after having been declared guilty of entering military territory and communicating secret information to the enemy."

But before he died, he had supplied the Israelis with the

complete plan of the Syrian fortifications on the Golan Heights, the movements of all the troops toward the frontiers, the delivery by the Soviets of 200 T 54-type tanks, the Syrian attack plans for upper Galilee, the first photos of Soviet Mig 21 fighters, and the plan for diverting the waters of the Jordan. He had forewarned his government of all the plots and all the coups d'état, even of the Syrian attempts to get rid of King Hussein of Jordan. He was acquainted with the secret cells of the Syrian army, with the Soviets' penetration of its inner counsel, and with the officers they used for this purpose.

Cohen sometimes abandoned his adopted role as a rich Syrian merchant, friendly with officers and men of power, to return to his wife and three children, with whom he would spend a few days. During his last stay he took his wife to the Club Meditérranée in Qisarya, where I have stayed myself. They hardly remember him there, except for his mania for photography. During his trips, under his cover as director of an export-import company, he would change his face, his passport, and his nationality, in Munich or Geneva or wherever, and then leave for Israel. It was during his last trip that he was apparently spotted by the Soviet secret services. The head of the Syrian secret service, Colonel Suweidani, later said that a goniometric radio car had localized his broadcasts to Israel. It is true—but it is also true that the Syrian secret service had been put on its guard against Cohen by its Soviet advisers.

The intelligence war, like all the subversive activities of the Palestinian commandos, took on a new aspect in 1968 as a result of the interventions of the Soviets. General Yariv was not yet done with spending sleepless nights on the cot in his office.

Mirages For General Hod

The principal Arab countries—Syria, Egypt, and Iraq—have adopted Soviet military doctrines completely, finding them rather suited to their national temperaments. The Israeli general staff, on the contrary, does not align itself with any school, or rather takes from all schools the doctrines that are useful to it and that can be adapted to the very special conditions of the country, conditions that arise, above all, from its geography and from the special nature of its population.

The Soviet doctrine can be summed up as simplicity on the lower echelons, complexity on the higher echelons. Battle plans are conceived in such a way as to avoid all sudden change and all improvisation, particularly in combat. Orders are clear. Very little initiative is left to junior officers. This doctrine suits the Russian soldier from the steppes or from the Central Asia Far Eastern republics, who is not on a very high intellectual or technical level. Matériel that is strongly built, extremely simple and easy to use is adapted to such a doctrine.

By contrast, at the brigade level and even more at the division level—at which all strategic and logistical problems are resolved—the Russians have competent trained officers, graduates of the leading military schools. They are accustomed to dealing with field commanders who are in effect, simply drovers of men. These excellent chess players who constitute the Soviet general staff move the pawns around the board—pawns who are not expected to have ideas but only to obey and to fight.

The Arab armies lack staff colonels and generals not only of quality but even of elementary competence. Following Soviet tactics, it is they, however, from whom all initiative must come. Yet at the very first setback they lose confidence and abandon their troops.

The whole of Soviet doctrine is centered on the offensive. When a unit is forced on to the defensive, it is considered only a momentary pause before a further advance. All the tactics of the Russian tank forces (tactics perfected by the German General Guderian) are based on the breakthrough. After a massive concentration of artillery fire on a very limited zone, the tanks open up a breach which the mechanized infantry then widens.

The Russians have, then, supplied the Arab countries with matériel suitable for such tactics: tanks, artillery, assault planes, armored troop carriers, and numerous half-tracks. Today their rotting hulks stretch for miles along the Jerusalem–Tel Aviv road. But the Arabs, except for the Jordanian legion founded by the British, haven't the slightest offensive spirit. The Egyptians viewed the Sinai as an impassable barrier, just as the Syrians regarded the Golan Heights. Consequently they deployed in a defensive system units basically organized for offensive action.

The entire Israeli doctrine, essentially pragmatic, is based on offense and lightning warfare. Offensive warfare is necessary because the state of Israel is only a very narrow strip of land that allows the army no room for retreat; in the Israeli army they say, "We have conquered our country in length but not in breadth." All of Israel's nerve centers—airfields, arms factories, arsenals, power plants—were, before the Six-Day War, not only vulnerable to bombing by enemy aircraft but also within range of the enemy artillery. Jordanian Long Tom cannons bombarded the center of

Tel Aviv without difficulty. Lightning warfare is imperative because the country's economic resources do not permit a long drawn-out conflict. Mobilization of 12 percent of the young and active population (300,000 out of 2.2 million inhabitants in 1967) paralyzes the country. And lightning warfare is also a must because intensively trained soldiers, accustomed to going without sleep, to improvising incessantly, and to fighting one against ten cannot last more than a month without risking collapse. Blocked on the land side, the Israelis, in case of a siege, can hope to receive supplies only by sea. Yet their navy is weak and cannot guarantee the freedom of their coasts. The Egyptians possess a surface navy and a submarine fleet whose tonnage is fourteen times that of Israel's navy.

On top of everything there is a political reason that makes lightning warfare an absolute necessity. Admiral Barjot has written in the *Revue Maritime:*

In a world in which the number of independent nations is multiplying, in which nationalist movements hostile to the West are evolving, in which racial and religious questions are involved, in which sordid interests dominate the decisions of even the most reliable allies, we must move very quickly. The plan of attack must enable us to overcome rapidly all opposition, not only military, but also political.

The Israelis were once forced by concerted political action of the great powers to abandon their conquests in the Sinai. But in 1967 they acted so quickly—and the Arab leaders showed themselves so stupid—that they were able to help themselves to everything they wanted before anyone had time to stop them.

Unlike the Russians and the Arabs, the Israeli generals know they can count on men, even in the very lowest ranks, who are intelligent, imaginative, and on a very high level of technical proficiency. Every soldier can replace his platoon leader, every platoon leader his captain, and every captain his colonel. There is thus every reason to permit maximum initiative in the field, provided, of course, that the troops are kept informed of the general staff's plans and intentions.

It is for this reason that the soldiers are continually informed of what is happening and the junior officers briefed by General Yariv's services just as if they might at any moment be going to take over direction of the battle—which has happened, notably on the Golan Heights, where one batallion was commanded by a private.

Because of Israel's limited territory and the concentration of its population and industry, the general staff is obliged to wage war elsewhere, that is, on neighboring territory.

The small extent of this territory singularly limits the possibility of constructing airfields. Also Israeli pilots would have only five aerodromes at their disposition for operations against the twenty five Arab bases. Enemy radar can easily cover the whole of Israeli territory, severely reducing the Israeli air force's freedom of action. (Ben Elissar and Schiff, *La guerre*).

The Israeli army was thus conceived as a shock force capable of invading enemy territory very rapidly and suddenly. Everything was subordinated, first to the air force, then to the tanks and the paratroopers.

As for the defense of the territory, it has to be ensured by the self-defense organizations provided by all frontier kibbutzim and all the Nahal military colonies. In this domain one rule is absolute: A kibbutz or Nahal colony that is attacked must defend itself alone, without hope of reinforcements. The regular army has other missions.

This shock and invasion force can be effective only if the sky above it is empty of enemy aircraft. The battlefields are always deserts, where it is practically impossible to camouflage concentrations of units. A column of tanks on a road amid the sands is too easy a target for aircraft. This invasion force also needs its air force for support in attacking enemy fortifications that are difficult to reduce and to redress the balance vis-à-vis forces that are always superior in manpower and almost always in matériel. Without mastery of the skies, lightning warfare can drag itself out. For time is against Israel. Against numbers there exists a defense—the quality of men and their training but against time there is none.

One might say that, whereas the frontier kibbutzim and military colonies are the shield of Israel—a fragile shield, for very few colonies are fortified—the paratroopers and the tank corps are its spear and the airforce its spearhead.

OPERATION FOCUS

This spearhead apparently knows its job. On Monday June 5, at 7:45 A.M., the Israeli air force, flying low over the waves to avoid the enemy radar, circled around and attacked all the airfields of the Sinai and the Nile delta from the rear, launching Operation Focus. Four hundred planes were destroyed on the ground. Thanks to a bomb "invented" by an ingenious engineer, every one of the landing fields was put out of commission. This bomb is dropped from a low altitude (about 300 feet); it is delayed by a retrorocket to allow the plane that drops it time to get away before it explodes. A booster rocket and its own rotary movement permit it to bury itself like a screw in the thick asphalt of the runway. Some of these bombs explode at once and others at irregular intervals thereafter; clearing the runways thus becomes a difficult and dangerous operation. The craters dug by the explosions are three yards deep and four yards wide. Even planes that were not hit could thus not take off. Nineteen bases were destroyed in this manner, even the one at Luxor, in Upper Egypt, where eight Tupolev 16 bombers had taken refuge.

Sixteen hours after the attack on the enemy bases was launched General Mordechai Hod, commander in chief of the air force, was able to issue the following victory communiqué:

During the day of June 5 we confronted the air forces of Egypt, Jordan, Syria, and Iraq. In the course of the day we destroyed about 400 enemy aircraft, as follows:

EGYPT: About 300 aircraft, including 30 Tu 16 (Tupolev) heavy bombers, 27 Il 28 (Ilyushin) medium bombers, 12 Su 7 (Sukhoi) fighter-bombers recently delivered to Egypt, 90 Mig 21s, 20 Mig 19s, 75 Mig 17s, 32 transport planes and helicopters. About twenty of these planes were shot down in aerial combat; the others were destroyed on the ground.

SYRIA: Fifty-two aircraft destroyed: thirty Mig 21s, twenty Mig 17s, two Il 27 medium bombers.

JORDAN: Twenty Hunter fighters and seven transport planes and helicopters.

IRAQ: Following the attack by a formation of Iraqi planes on several Israeli concentrations, we bombed Base H 3 in Iraq and there destroyed six Mig 21s and three Hunters.

In the course of the same day, we incurred the following losses: Nineteen pilots, including eight dead and eleven missing. Among the missing, several were captured by the enemy.

The Arab countries' forces had been as follows: Egypt had thirty Tu 16 bombers, forty Il 28 medium bombers, twelve Su 17 fighter-bombers, one hundred thirty Mig 21s, eighty Mig 19s, one hundred Mig 17s, and fifty Mig 15s. Syria had thirty-six Mig 21s, sixty Mig 17s, forty Mig 15s, and fifteen Il 28 bombers. Iraq had forty Hunter (British) fighter-bombers, fifty Migs (17s, 19s, and 21s), and ten Il 28 medium bombers. Jordan had twelve Hunter (British) fighters, sixteen Vampire bombers, thirty-six Starfighter (American) fighter-bombers, and four Alouette (French) helicopters.

The air strength of Israel was composed of seventy-two Mirage III Cs, twenty-four Super Mystères, forty Mystère IV As, forty Ouragans, twenty-four Vautours, twelve Nord-Atlases, five Super Frelon and four Alouette helicopters, as well as fourteen Sikorsky helicopters made in America but delivered to Israel by West Germany, and sixty Fouga-Magister training craft manufactured in Israel under a French license.

The following planes participated in the attack on Arab bases: the Mirages, the Mystères and Super Mystères, the Vautours, the old Ouragans, and the Fouga-Magisters, which are theoretically only training planes. In all, 150 planes took part. Only twelve fast combat planes were kept in reserve to defend the entire country. It was a dangerous choice.

By the end of the Six-Day War 450 Arab aircraft had been destroyed, 61 of them in aerial combat. The Israelis lost, according to the figures that General Hod himself gave me: forty combat planes and six Fouga-Magisters destroyed by antiaircraft guns, one Mystère, and one Super Mystère shot down in combat by Mig 21s, one Mirage forced to sacrifice itself to protect four Vautours being attacked by eight Mig 21s.

By the same date Egypt had lost 338 planes, Syria 61, Jordan 29, Iraq 23 planes, and Lebanon 1.

DIFFICULT BEGINNINGS

The origins of the Israeli air force were, for all that, very modest. When the U.N. voted for partition of Palestine and recognized the Jews' right to national independence in November 1947, the Jewish air force was practically nonexistent and comprised only eleven sport or training craft, including two Tiger-Moths (British), three Taylor craft, one Auster, and one fast Dragon.

Some of these planes belonged to the Palestinian Aviation Club, others to individuals. They served to carry provisions and weapons, as well as to evacuate wounded men, and were based on British soil. It is to the Haganah, the Jewish self-defense organization, that the Jews owe the creation, at that time, of an "aerial service." This embryonic service soon numbered thirty-seven crewmen, who knew how to take care of the planes and to fly them: thirteen Palestinian Jews who had served with the R.A.F. in World War II, eleven Palestinian Jews trained by the Haganah in Palestine, two Palestinian Jews who were amateur pilots, nine foreign Jews (mainly Americans) and two foreign pilots of the Roman Catholic faith.

The Haganah representative in New York, Yehuda Arazi, was able first to raise the necessary funds and then to purchase ten Curtiss 46s and three Constellations. At that time the United States government was selling vast amounts of "obsolete" matériel for 2 percent of its cost. The Curtiss 46s thus cost $5,000 apiece as surplus and the Constellations $15,000.

The pilots, all volunteers, were trained in California, on the ranch of Eleanor Rudnick, who owned a private airfield. A small private company called Service Airway, Inc., was purchased to serve as a front for the secret buying of planes, parts, and weapons and the shipment of all this matériel to Israel. This company later became the Lineas Aereas de Panama, for in Panama everything is simpler if one knows whose palms to cross with silver.

But for the time being the planes remained in the United States. Another Haganah agent, Freddie, a former colonel in the R.A.F., took advantage of the friendly cooperation of his wartime buddies to purchase British bombers, but they were seized at Rhodes just as they were about to make the last short hop to Tel Aviv: He fell back on the American stock piles in Germany, and was able to dispatch twenty-seven Nordsman planes to Israel. But the Nordsman is a spotter plane. He still lacked fighters and bombers.

Against Israel the Arabs had lined up a genuine military air force. The Egypt of King Farouk possessed forty fighters (mostly Spitfires), forty light bombers (converted Dakotas), and twenty transport planes, as well as about fifteen reconnaissance or training craft. Syria had fifteen Harvards converted into light bombers, and Iraq had six fighters and six Anson bombers. On May 15, 1948, the Arab planes were able to invade the sky over the new State of Israel and to subject Tel Aviv, Haifa, and other cities and towns to intense bombing.

Israeli inferiority did not last long, however. First, the spotter planes were armed—with hand grenades and locally manufactured bombs. When the first 110-pound bomb emerged from the workshops the crewmen viewed it with some apprehension. It was, indeed, something to give one pause: Imagine an egg-shaped object armed with a delayed-action fuse that triggered by pulling a metal wire. "How does one drop this bomb?" asked one of the pilots. The weapons engineer, who was American, answered, in English, "You push it." "Push, push, Pushkin," the pilot chanted, and from then on 110-pound bombs were nicknamed Pushkins, which may seem rather poetic for an engine of death. It was certainly a dangerous weapon to handle.

The Curtisses and Constellations bought from American surplus were shipped via Panama to Catania in Sicily and then to Israel. Meanwhile the Czechoslovakians agreed to sell Israel twelve Messerschmitts, each equipped with two 20 mm. guns and two machine guns. They were dispatched in parts. The pilots were trained in Czechoslovakia. The first two of these pilots had scarcely entered combat when they downed two Egyptian bombers.

But Israel could not be content with these very short range fighters. Bombers were needed, and so four B17 Flying Fortresses that had been converted into transport planes were purchased. Only three of them were able to take off, but they had to be rearmed (with twelve machine guns and three tons of bombs).

The purchase of four Beaufighter light bombers posed more problems. Colonel Benjamin Kagan, who was one of the directors of the "production" that enabled them to leave, tells the story in his book *Combat secret pour Israël:*

. . . it therefore appeared to be impossible, without a firm alibi, to remove the bombers from the soil of England.
It was then that fortune smiled on us, in the form of a young and charming New Zealand actress, the friend of one of the pilots Zur had signed up. This young woman had spoken to her friend about a film project glorifying the exploits of New Zealanders in the war. Little by little, a strange idea took hold in Emmanuel

Zur's mind. It was the simplest of ideas: to undertake the production of a film about the activities of New Zealand pilots in the war; then, in the logical unfolding of a sequence especially written for this purpose, the pilots would take off in the Beaufighters and disappear from the skies of England along with the fictitious production.

Thanks to our friends in the British cinema world, a production company was duly set us, and, behind this facade, we were able to proceed freely to hire not ordinary actors but the pilots we needed.

Came the day when the four Beaufighters, on the ground, confronted the movie lights. The scene was shot only once. The planes took off and disappeared. Thanks to the complicity of the producer, the authorities were not notified of the disappearance of the planes until after the latter had landed peacefully at the airport of Ajaccio, which had just been put at our disposal again.

Spitfires, also bought in Czechoslovakia, have a flight range of only 200 miles, and getting them to Israel posed problems that seemed insurmountable. The operation, organized under the most precarious conditions and known by the code name Velveta, made it possible to provide the Jewish state with about twenty combat aircraft.

This air force was, no doubt, nothing more than a conglomeration of leftover planes, but in the war of independence it was of prime importance. It played a decisive role in the battles of Galilee and the Negev and in the destruction, during the summer of 1948, of the airfield of El 'Arish.

By the end of 1948 its superiority was incontestable. The Israeli air force consisted of more than seventy combat planes, a few real bombers, and some transport planes converted into bombers. Messerschmitts, Spitfires, and Flying Fortresses sat side by side on the former British bases with Austers, Taylor crafts, several Douglas DC 5s, a Lockheed Hudson, Nordsman planes of Canadian origin, four Skymasters, several C 46 Commandos, some Harvards, one reconnaissance Nord 1203, Beaufighters, and even a Constellation transport. The force numbered about 100 pilots, as well as 2,000 men in the ground crews, the repair shops, and military and civilian personnel of the general staff. Its role was so important that Ben-Gurion, then Prime Minister and Minister of Defense, wrote, "The fact that the state of Israel exists today and that its frontiers extend from Dan to Elath is due in great part to the Israeli air force. We would surely not have been able to repel the Arab invasion and to liberate the Negev without our air superiority."

But, even though they rendered merited homage to the air force, Israeli leaders were still not disposed to grant it the position that it deserved. There were several reasons why. The first was psychological: To Ben-Gurion, as to the "money men" Levi Eshkol and Kaplan, the air force was only a fairy tale. They preferred things that were solid and firmly anchored to the ground, tanks, for example. The other, more serious, reason was economic. For a long time the enormous budget that the experts demanded to transform the Haganah's "aerial service" into a modern air force came up against a stubborn refusal from leaders overwhelmed by economic problems. The first commanders in chief of the air force lacked experience in the field: In 1950 General Shlomo Shemir, a former commander of the navy, was appointed to the post; he was succeeded in 1951 by a specialist in armored units, General Haim Laskov. The Israeli air force under Laskov's direction devoted itself to ground tasks: modernizing air bases, constructing new runways, and building quarters for the crewmen. He did, however, provide the air force with a network of training schools and centers. Above all, he concerned himself with the professional instruction of ground crews, systematizing training, and establishment of strict discipline. It was under his aegis that Israeli pilots were first sent to England to train on Meteors, which the government in Jerusalem had finally decided to acquire.

The appointment in 1953 of General Dan Tolkovski, formerly of the R.A.F., was a decisive turning point for the air force. Tolkovski went beyond profound changes in the Israeli air force itself; he also significantly changed the high command's attitude toward it and introduced a genuine air strategy. But, in order to put his views across, Tolkovski had to fight very energetically, first against the civil authorities and then against the army's chief of staff, who was none other than General Moshe Dayan. It is curious that Dayan, who had just worked out the strategy of reprisals, still underestimated the role of aviation in modern warfare.

Tolkovski's air strategy boiled down to three points: First, the air force had to be provided with up-to-date military aircraft, for modern warfare cannot be waged without squadrons of fighters and interceptors, to protect the territory against all enemy air attacks, and fighter-bombers, to carry the war into enemy territory. Second, when a country as small as Israel is surrounded on all sides by hostile neighbors and its urban centers are within range of any enemy fighter or bomber, speed and efficiency of its aircraft are strategic imperatives. Third, speed is a function of the caliber of the planes at the air force's disposal and of the training level of their crews; efficiency, for a country like Israel, whose financial resources are in any case minimal, requires uniformity of aircraft and maximum utilization of planes in a given period of time.

If the Israeli air force wanted to answer the needs of national defense, it had to dump its hodgepodge of planes of all types and all origins and to acquire a homogeneous fleet of planes belonging to the same aeronautical "family." According to Tolkovski, each plane had to be usable in a number of different tasks. The distinctions among combat plane, tactical support plane, and bomber were thus to be eliminated: The Israeli aircraft, all of the same basic type, would theoretically be employed in different missions.

Little by little, Tolkovski ended by getting his views accepted. And it was on the occasion of the reapprochement with France—the work of Deputy Minister of Defense Shimon Peres and French Ambassador to Israel Monsieur

Gilbert—that Tolkovski's objectives finally began to be realized. After having made contact with the leading circles of French aviation and with certain individuals in the French government who favored closer Franco-Israeli friendship ties, Peres returned to Israel with a report sure to arouse Tolkovski's enthusiasm: France was prepared to supply ultramodern jet aircraft, radar, and auxiliary electronic equipment in large quantities. But it seemed that agreement on this program could not be reached without overcoming obstacles on both sides. On the Israeli side months and months of discussion were necessary before the government agreed to the demands of Tolkovski and Peres: the purchase, not of a half-dozen, but of several dozen, supersonic planes. On the French side there was similar resistance. Despite the signed letter of agreement with the government of Pierre Mendès-France in 1954, which stipulated the sale to Israel of a formation of Ouragans, six Mystère IIs and twelve Mystère IVs, more than a year of negotiations had to pass before the first Ouragans landed in Israel. The Quai d'Orsay [the French Foreign Ministry] is hostile on principle. There is on the Quai an old tradition of friendship with the Moslem countries of the Middle East dating from the agreements concluded between Francis I and the Great Turk. This tradition was strengthened when former French Ambassador to Cairo Maurice Couve de Murville became Minister of Foreign Affairs.

Furthermore, the French air force was reluctant to modify its own working plans in order to deliver twelve Mystère IVs as well. In spite of these difficulties, the Ouragans landed in Israel in October 1955 and the first Mystère IVs in April 1956. All these deliveries were carried out with the greatest discretion. The massive arrival of French matériel on the eve of the Sinai campaign in 1956 propelled the Israeli air force into the supersonic era. Israel received, within a few months, sixty Mystère IVs, some Nord-Atlases, some Dakotas, and even, at the end of the Sinai campaign, a formation of Vautour bombers. What a difference from the motley armada of 1948–1949! Israeli pilots, trained in France and then in Israel, quickly mastered the subtleties of modern aviation technology. And so Tolkovski's prayers were partly fulfilled: The Israeli air force was supplied with modern aircraft and highly qualified pilots trained to carry out the most diversified missions.

This new air force, though better adapted to defend the country, was unable, however, to take on the Egyptian air force in 1956. At Ben-Gurion's request, the R.A.F. provided the "aerial umbrella," and the Israeli pilots were ordered not to risk their planes and their lives over Egyptian territory or, rather, over the Suez Canal. Their mission consisted solely of engaging the enemy over the Sinai and lending tactical support to General Dayan's tanks. In this respect, they often played a decisive role. The Dakotas and Nord-Atlases from France dropped paratroopers on the banks of the Suez Canal and at Sharm el-Sheikh. For the first time, the Mystère IVs had a chance to prove themselves against Egyptian Vampires and Mig 15s; they were highly successful.

Today Israeli pilots claim that the Treaty of Sèvres, signed by France, Britain, and Israel, which forbade the Israeli air force to cross the Suez Canal, prevented the latter from demonstrating what it is capable of: annihilation of the Egyptian air force on its own. It nevertheless remains a fact that the Sinai campaign confirmed Dan Tolkovski's doctrine. His theory of paired aircraft as the basic unit of combat and tactical support was strongly reinforced in this test. In Israel all reconnaissance, support, pursuit, and bombing missions are, in fact, planned for units of two aircraft (not four, six, eight or twelve, as in other countries). The second plane of each pair protects the first as it goes into combat or, if necessary, covers its retreat. This tactic, which proved effective in the Sinai, was carried still further during the Six-Day War. Starting with the attack of June 5, the Israeli planes flew in formations of four, each formation consisting of two pairs of planes. The first pair engaged in combat, while the second guaranteed its security; the second pair went into combat only when the first had finished its attack.

STRATEGY OF THE ISRAELI AIR FORCE

To General Tolkovski's successor Ezer Weizmann, appointed in 1958, fell the task of transforming the Israeli air force once and for all into an "iron fist." Tolkovski had created a modern air arm adapted to the particular needs of his country; Weizmann developed and perfected the instrument that his predecessor had bequeathed him. Ezer Weizmann is the nephew of the first President of the Republic, the scientist who, for services rendered to the Allied cause, obtained from Lord Balfour the famous declaration creating a Jewish home in Israel. He is Israel's *enfant terrible,* a powerful and explosive giant who thinks clearly, says what he thinks, and doesn't care who hears him. In May 1966 he threatened to throw his stripes in the face of Levi Eshkol, whose wait-and-see policy as President of the Council Weizmann deplored.

Though a former R.A.F. pilot, he had nevertheless shot down in aerial combat two British planes that were flying over Israeli territory. At the moment, he is the operational chief of the air force, and he gets around in an old Spitfire, which he has painted black with two red stripes, perhaps in memory of the two British comrades whom he taught to respect the new Israeli state.

General Weizmann has one limitless passion—the air force —and his incisive remarks on the subject are celebrated: "To be a pilot in Israel is to be a pioneer in the same way as the farmers in the kibbutzim" (he himself was a pioneer in a kibbutz on Mount Carmel); "The best men belong in the air force"; "The guard of Israel is mounted 40,000 feet up."

It was he who received and tested the first jet aircraft that France dispatched to Israel. He was grateful, and he sent the general staff of the French air force the first motion pictures ever taken of a fight between an Israeli Mirage and an Egyptian Mig. They constituted proof, on film, that the air-to-air missiles with which the Soviet plane was equipped could not hit a Mirage if the latter's pilot knew how to maneuver in a certain way.

In August 1962, when Egypt tested its first ground-to-ground missile, Weizmann set forth in the Israeli newspaper *Maariv* his views on the absolutely basic role of Israeli aviation. In the light of the Six-Day War these views stand out in sharp relief and demonstrate clearly that Israel's "lightning warfare" is the fruit of a policy that was thought through ahead.

So long as the war that threatens Israel is a conventional war and not a nuclear one, the ground-to-ground missile with a range of 250 to 300 miles that Egypt has at her disposal cannot take the place of the air force, either in Egypt or in Israel. The missiles can carry explosives into enemy territory and can devastate civilian centers. But, to end the war victoriously, it will be necessary to rely on a fast and effective air force. To protect itself from the Egyptian missiles, Israel must improve and reinforce its air force without letup.

The missile, which constitutes a deterrent to war, demands astronomical investments that threaten to lead a small country, with limited financial means, to the brink of bankruptcy. Israel needs a long-term deterrent that can guarantee victory. The defense of Israel consequently requires continued efforts to provide ourselves with the most modern and best-equipped air force in this whole region. The advent of the Egyptian missiles has not changed this doctrine in any particular; we must apply it all the more and consecrate all our efforts to the air force.

The primary task of that force consists of demolishing the enemy's air power. Once this task is accomplished, when the skies of Israel have been made inviolable, the air force can devote itself to its second task, lending assistance to the ground forces.

The first task is the function of several factors, of which the most important is that of surprise. The first country to launch a surprise attack stands the chance of achieving air supremacy and thus of gaining victory. Egypt not only possesses missiles that enable it right now to launch a surprise attack and to wreak serious damage on civilian and military bases; it also has at its disposal three formations of bombers, eight of fighters, and three of transport. In other words, Egypt possesses about 100 Mig 19s and 50 Mig 21s. Sooner or later, these planes will be armed with air-to-air missiles; it is probable that they will also be equipped in the near future with air-to-ground missiles. Egypt will, furthermore, receive ground-to-air missiles, to protect its territory against invasion.

Under these conditions, the Israeli air force will have to fight for hours and perhaps days to gain aerial supremacy. Meanwhile, the rear will be uncovered and will necessarily serve as a target for ground-to-ground missiles and enemy bombs.

But another factor must be taken into consideration, a factor known in technical jargon as "absorption capacity": that is, a country's capacity to sustain aerial bombings. The fact is that Egypt's absorption capacity is greater than Israel's. To grasp this, it suffices to compare the extent of Egyptian territory with that of Israel. Egypt has infinitely more opportunities to disperse its military and civil bases throughout the whole of its territory. In the case in which the enemy has air superiority, we must at all costs keep that superiority from being prolonged for more than a day to a day and a half. The idea of not obtaining air superiority until after the first phase, during which our strategic points will have been devastated—this idea is absolutely inadmissible and unrealistic.

We are consequently forced to provide ourselves with a thorough antiaircraft defense, not only aircraft that possess what is needed to paralyze enemy planes on the ground or shoot them down in combat but also a protection system ranging from air-raid shelters to the most up-to-date antiaircraft weapons. Only an effective protective system can create an impenetrable defense curtain against enemy aircraft, which will aproach from the four quarters of the compass.

The third factor, also decisive, consists of the number of missions our aircraft will be able to complete within a given time in comparison with the number of enemy missions in the same period.

Put another way, this means the number of effective combat sorties that each of our planes will be able to execute. That number is a function of the quality of the planes, their quantity, their speed, the number and location of our air bases, the level of upkeep of the aircraft, and the competence of our pilots.

The Israeli air force is quantitatively inferior to the Egyptian air force. It can permit itself to remain so if it is nevertheless capable of accomplishing at least as many missions as the enemy; if not, I doubt that we can obtain air superiority.

The integration of strength is a final factor on which the outcome of the battle depends. We need a plane capable of penetrating Egyptian antiaircraft defenses, carrying out bombing raids in spite of radar and avoiding hits by ground-to-air and air-to-air missiles. It is a question, in other words, of a plane that is fast but also capable of carrying bombs. From now on it is inconceivable for us to use outmoded bombers, even those that carry eight to ten tons of bombs. It is true that an aircraft carrying a big load of bombs is very useful for the support of ground troops. But we cannot allow ourselves to maintain three distinct air forces, one for tactical support, another for combat, and a third for bombing raids. We need the most modern airplane.

The entire tactics of the Israeli air force are summed up in these words. It is astonishing that the Arab states, including Egypt and its Russian protector, not only have not familiarized themselves with them but have not profited from them in the least.

Truly, what a strange country is Israel, where people shut you out of the battlefield as if it were a secret weapon yet the head of the air force publishes in a newspaper with a large circulation all the secrets of his country's aerial strategy!

The Israelis have made great progress in increasing the missions flown by their planes. The Six-Day War attests to this increase. In June 1967 the French Mirages completed more than twelve missions a day, and the interval between Mirage missions was reduced by the ground crews to seven minutes, whereas the acceptable interval under NATO standards is twenty minutes. At one Israeli air base, a pilot even told me that this interval had been reduced to four minutes and fifty-five seconds. *Aviation Magazine* of August 15, 1967, noted in this connection, "The 140 to 150 first-wave attack planes at Israel's disposal did the work of 300 to 600 planes."

According to General Weizmann, these fast, ultramodern aircraft, capable of executing record numbers of missions, were to carry the war beyond Israel's borders and into the heart of the Arab countries: to the Suez Canal, to the Jordan, to Damascus and Cairo. Israel's sole "defense" is precisely in such an offensive. The sky is Israel's only open dimension: "Altitude and range are our strategic depth," Weizmann says.

From 1958 to 1967 Weizmann and his successor, General Mordechai Hod, who became commandant for the air force in April 1966, made every effort to modernize Israeli avaiation and to maximize its operational effectiveness. Until the Six-Day War, this modernization continued to be channeled through France. While maintaining the matériel previously delivered by France—that is, the Mystère IVs and even the Ouragans—Israel strove to acquire ultramodern fighters, the only ones capable of satisfying its strategic needs. It was a question of progressing from Mach 1 to Mach 2, in order to match the Mig 21s that were being delivered in great quantities to the Arab countries by the U.S.S.R. The first truly supersonic plane delivered to the Israeli air force was the Super Mystère; the Mystère IV reached supersonic speeds only in dives. From France Israel ordered an entire formation of Super Mystères, which were immediately incorporated into the air force's combat units and which headed the military parade on Independence Day in 1959.

Although the purchase of twenty-four Super Mystère B 2s, ratified by the Fourth Republic and completed in the first days of the Fifth Republic, did not really raise any problems, things did not go so smoothly with the Mirage IIIs, which constituted, in the view of Israeli experts, the best answer to the Mig 21. Although the general staff of the French army and French manufacturers of the Mirage agreed to supply

Israel and an agreement in principle was signed by Shimon Peres and the French Minister of War Pierre Messmer, the Quai d'Orsay categorically opposed this sale in 1961. As in 1954–1955, months of talks were required before a conclusion could be reached, and the Quai, anxious to improve France's relations with the Arab countries, meanwhile refused to deliver to Israel one of the best supersonic fighters in Europe. After an interministerial meeting attended by Prime Minister Georges Pompidou, Messmer, and Foreign Minister Couve de Murville, General de Gaulle finally pronounced himself in favor of the sale of the Mirages to Israel. Six squadrons of twelve planes were delivered to Israel before 1967. The Six-Day War thus witnessed the triumph of the French Mirage over the Mig 21, as the Sinai campaign had witnessed, though in less overwhelming fashion, the victory of the Mystère over the Mig 17. In June 1967 the Israeli air force was almost entirely equipped with French matériel. It reflected Tolkovski's and Weizmann's insistence that it be constituted of diverse functions. The Israeli helicopters, radar installations, and electronic equipment were also of French origin.

Israel, anxious to increase the effectiveness of its aerial forces to the maximum, did not stop at acquiring matériel abroad but transformed and perfected it in the light of its own strategic needs. For instance, the Atar engine, with which the Mirage is equipped, underwent certain alterations in Israel. The Israeli command also refused to equip its Mirages exclusively with air-to-air missiles of the Matra type, but chose to use 30 mm. guns as well. The Matra missile was outrageously expensive ($30,000 to $50,000 each), but the French manufacturers maintained that, at speeds in excess of Mach 2 (the Mirage can attain Mach 2.5), no pilot could aim a gun and fire it effectively at a supersonic enemy plane. The Israelis claimed the opposite. After making a series of alterations in the Mirage, they armed it with two 30 mm. guns. The Six-Day War proved them right. All the enemy planes destroyed in aerial combat were downed by guns, except for a single one destroyed by a Matra missile.

Israeli aviators also learn to make their matériel last. Mystère IVs are built to last for 900 flight hours; in Israel, some have logged 2,000 hours. And what can one say about the old Ouragans that are still in use?

The French Mirages proved to be better than the Mig 21s. In August 1966 a Mig 21, the very latest product of the Soviet aircraft industry, whose characteristics and performance capabilities were still unknown in the West, landed in perfect condition on an airfield in Israel, with its Iraqi pilot at the controls. (It was said that the pilot was a Kurd and a Christian, that he felt persecuted, that he had acted for money—$200,000, or even $300,000. But the truth is General Yariv's secret.) The Mig 21 was given the identification number 007, in memory of James Bond, and was put through a series of trials. Mirage pilots put in hundreds of training hours in it. Here is what they learned:

Despite the mediocrity of its exterior, due to negligence in the finishing work, it is an excellent high-altitude fighter. Unlike the Mirage, whose fuselage is smooth and fine, the outer surface of the Mig is sprinkled with thousands of rivets. The Mirage maneuvers and dives infinitely better than the Mig, which responds more slowly to controls in combat. The Mirage attains an effective speed of Mach 2.15 to Mach 2.2, whereas the Mig is incapable of exceeding a maximum speed of Mach 2.

The visibility in the cockpit of the Mirage—practically 360 degrees—is infinitely superior to that of the Mig. The protective sheathing of the Mig's cockpit is, on the other hand, thicker than that of the Mirage.

The firing rate of the Mig's gun—about 600 30 mm. cartridges a minute—is one and a half to two times lower than that of our guns. But the Mig, unlike the Israel Mirage, is permanently armed with "Atoll" air-to-air missiles with infrared guidance mechanisms.

The ignition system of the Mig is based on gasoline. This system increases the autonomy of the aircraft, which can take off without the need for auxiliary ignition. But, on the other hand, it necessarily involves the terrible danger of explosion in flight, if the ignition gas tank is hit by a shellburst.

It is the quality of the pilots and their training, more than the matériel, that makes for the excellence of the Israeli air force, however. The future pilot is selected from among the young men who have just received their secondary-school diplomas, corresponding to the French *baccalauréat*. He signs up for five years and six months in the air force. Then he undergoes a long series of physical and psychological tests: the first elimination trials. During a period of eighteen months he is then turned into a toughened paratrooper and receives all the training given to shock troops: the second round of eliminations. The percentage of those chosen is considerably reduced. At this point the future pilot knows how to elude capture, find his directions, and defend himself if he has to eject over enemy territory. When he is called upon to give support to ground troops, he will know his comrades' fighting methods thoroughly and his own actions will be more effective for it. Final recruiting of aviators generally nets a high percentage of men from the kibbutzim and the moshavim (collectivist villages). General Mordechai Hod, the current commandant of the air force, came from a kibbutz himself, and the majority of the pilots are sabras, that is, native-born Israelis.

Since 1960 pilots have begun their training in a jet plane, the Fouga-Magister (more than 440 miles an hour at an altitude of 30,000 feet). This plane is now manufactured under license in Israel.

It is by his performance that the pilot's ultimate assignment is determined. The best men are trained on combat planes— Mirages, Super Mystères, Bautours; the rest become transport pilots. The training of a jet pilot costs around 1 million francs, an enormous sum for a small country that already must devote more than 11 percent of its total budget to its armed forces.

The moment that he is commissioned, the pilot goes on a permanent state of alert. It cannot be otherwise in an army that can be summoned at any moment to intervene on any front; he trains for both aerial combat and bombing attacks. These fliers establish regular kibbutzim around the air bases where they are assigned. They lead communal lives and marry very young. Many pilots are fathers at twenty. To test the speed of the base's often-complex functioning, the general staff frequently issues general alarms. Sometimes they require vast exercises that activate the entire complement of every single air base in the country. But the reprisal raids, which have not ceased since the end of the war, are still the best exercises.

VISIT TO AN AIR BASE

I was able to visit an air base about sixty miles from Tel Aviv and to have a talk with the pilots. They were, of course, on a state of alert. A few minutes later they were going to fly over Jordan with their planes loaded with bombs and napalm. They belonged to a squadron of Mystère IV "A"s, the first supersonic planes that Israel received; formerly a fighter-interceptor, it now serves as a ground-support plane and light bomber.

The base consists of some white barracks set among eucalyptus trees and the hangars where the planes are checked out, their bellies loaded with bombs. This squadron is both an operational 500-pound unit and a training unit for pilots. The average age of the men is between twenty-one and twenty-three years. The reserve pilots who come to take refresher courses are older; many fly for the national airline El Al, others live in kibbutzim but take advantage of the slightest pretext to come for further training. The squadron has fought well, and three Mystères have shot down a Mig 17, a Mig 21, and a Hunter (which is faster and better armed than the Mystère). The commandant of the unit, who is almost as young as his pilots, laughingly begins by de-molishing certain legends that were current during the Six-Day War, especially the one in which jet pilots, in order to bomb more accurately, let down their landing gear to slow themselves down.

"Nonsense," he tells me. "I was there; it would have been impossible and stupid. On the other hand, we did attack the El 'Arish base from thirty feet."

I ask him: "Why do most of the pilots come from kib-butzim?"

"It's not hard to figure. In the city, the family decides for the child. In the kibbutz, the child is free and decides every-thing for himself. There is a more highly developed sense of community in the kibbutzim than in the cities, for people there know just how great Israel's danger is and that one must fight incessantly to survive. So, even though the kib-butzim don't account for more than 3 or 4 percent of the country's population, they furnish 35 percent of the pilots."

"Do your victories depend on the quality of your aircraft —Mirages and so on?"

"On the quality of the pilots. Put an Israeli pilot in a Mig 21 and an Egyptian pilot in a Mirage, and the Israeli pilot will knock out the Egyptian every time.

"Listen carefully: During the Six-Day War, no enemy plane shot down a single Israeli plane in aerial combat. Every one of our aerial combats was a pursuit. Not once did any plane, even a Mig 21, face us head-on. We got them in the tail. [This is inaccurate: some Israeli planes were shot down in aerial combat—precisely three. But it is true, on the other hand, that all the Arab planes shot down in combat were fleeing.] The Arab pilots couldn't care less about their planes.

"Listen to this story that an Italian journalist told me. He was being transported by helicopter somewhere near the Suez by an Egyptian army pilot. The pilot misjudged his distance and crashed the plane. The journalist and the pilot weren't hurt too badly, but the craft was a wreck. The Italian

sympathized with the Egyptian, 'You poor guy, what are you going to do?'

" 'That's the third one I've smashed up this week,' said the other with a shrug. He looked as if he didn't give a damn, as if he didn't risk so much as a reprimand. Can you imagine that happening with us?

"The Egyptian pilots who ejected over the Sinai and parachuted down unharmed—do you think their buddies tried to rescue them? In some places it would have been easy. Not one. It didn't even occur to them.

"With us it's just the opposite; we do the impossible and risk our skins . . . and matériel to save a comrade. It's a sacred law."

Even so, they hold onto matériel; it's what they most lack.

Here is Moshe, a reservist doing his annual stint. He is thirty-one and looks like Nasser, with his height and his black moustache. He learned that war had broken out while he was at Heraklion, in Crete, crop-dusting with a little plane. In his Piper Cub he made it to Rhodes, then Cyprus, and finally arrived in sight of the Israeli coast. He was in danger of being shot down by his own country's antiaircraft or fighters, so he flew just above the waves. Fortunately, he was able to make radio contact with an El Al plane whose pilot he knew. The latter alerted the antiaircraft defense to let him pass. A few hours later he was at the controls of a Mystère and shot down a Syrian plane.

Here is Captain Abraham, a pleasant, quiet young man of twenty-six. He shot down a Mig 19 and a Mig 21, both "in the tail." He was flying a Mirage, and here he is supervising training on Mystères.

I ask him how he did it.

"It's very simple," he answers. "I've never forgotten the principle that they drum into you: 'When you go to fight, always think that the enemy pilot is better than you and then prove the opposite.' "

And here is——. He doesn't give his name. His buddies tell his story for him. He is twenty-three years old. He has *shot down six Mig 21s. He was wounded but escaped from the hospital and went up again in his Mirage.*

All the pilots assure me

• that their planes have not been modified or "souped up" in any way; they are the same as the ones used in France.

• that their training is easier to arrange than that of French pilots because Israel always enjoys excellent weather conditions and high visibility, so that it is possible to fly every day and to fly very low.

• that the Egyptian pilots are not really pilots; they know only how to make their planes fly.

• that in general the Arabs are afraid of going into combat in a plane.

• that there is not a single country in the world where airplanes are repaired as quickly as in Israel.

One of them assures me that, while bombing the Golan Heights, he was hit by antiaircraft and forced to make a pancake landing. The next morning the plane took off again.

The pilots are all very friendly. Not a single one reproaches me about those fifty Mirages that the Israelis have bought and paid for and that the French government has refused to deliver to them. But the question is burning on their tongues. It is their commander, General Mordechai Hod, who finally raises it with me.

"MOTTI" HOD SPEAKS

General Hod, whom everybody calls Motti, is a husky, phlegmatic fellow with a narrow face who at forty-one is losing his hair and sports a moustache. He is sunk deep in his armchair, as in a pilot's seat. I wait for him to stretch his long legs out on top of the table American-style, so little does this man seem made to sit quietly behind a desk.

He became a general at thirty-nine. He was the first pilot of the Haganah to be trained in a Piper Cub. At twenty he took his first lessons at an aviation club in Rome. No sooner was he on his own than he dived at the Vatican, which won him a stay behind bars.

I have hardly entered his office when he asks me, "And my Mirages?"

Everyone here seems to hold every individual Frenchman responsible for the policy of Charles de Gaulle. On my next visit to Israel I fully intend to have cards printed as follows:

"I have nothing to do with General de Gaulle: I disapprove of his domestic and foreign policies. I therefore beg you not to hold me or my countrymen who visit you in Israel responsible for Gaullist policy in the Middle East, for his grandiose schemes, or for his betrayals. Thank you."

Motti leans forward.

"What's going on in France? [It is at the end of the May 1968 disturbances.] What do the students want? Is de Gaulle going to quit? Do you think that if there's another government we'll get our Mirages? It's no longer 50 that we need but 100, for we had some losses during the Six-Day War. The Egyptian air force has been considerably reinforced, and with very modern matériel. It possesses more Mig 21s than in May 1967, and as it lost very few pilots. . . . They were eating breakfast when we destroyed their planes."

He waves a model of the new Mirage V under my nose.

"We're the ones who helped you perfect it. We asked that its electronic system be simplified and its jets strengthened so that it can carry a heavier bomb load while retaining the same flight range and not reducing its speed.

"This aircraft was perfected and made really operational thanks to the engagements our pilots fought and the lessons they learned. This new-model Mirage is partly of our own design—or at least the fruit of a very close collaboration— and de Gaulle is going to sell it to the Iraqis, who are our enemies, and he refuses to release the fifty that we have paid for under the pretext of an embargo on arms to the Middle

East, a one-sided embargo since Iraq is going to receive some—and Iraq is at war with us."

I raise my hands helplessly.

"Maybe the Americans will sell you other planes!"

"The Phantoms cost three times as much as the Mirages; they are more fragile and more complicated. We are used to French matériel. Michel Debré is now Foreign Minister. He doesn't detest us like Couve de Murville. Maybe we'll get our Mirages. Your strikes are going to cost a packet, and we Israelis pay for our planes in cash—and in dollars."

General Hod puts the model of the Mirage V down on his desk. I have no desire to stay too long on this ticklish subject. I ask, "How do you explain your crushing victory over the air forces of the Arab countries?"

"It was partly owing to the mistakes of the Arab pilots, mistakes they never stopped making from the opening of combat, namely, Monday, June 6, at 7:45. They lost all common sense, and they transformed a defeat into a disaster. And then everything went very well for us. Our pilots did even better in war than they had in training. Our plans were carried out 100 percent, in spite of all the factors that are not taken into account in an exercise, like antiaircraft, for example.

"We ought to have been content to destroy the Arab planes on the ground, but I insisted that my pilots confront Arab pilots in aerial combat, to get used to it, to put the permanent fear of God into the Arabs, and to gain confidence. It wasn't easy to force the Arabs into combat; they didn't have much stomach for it.

"During the entire Six-Day War, a third of our planes' sorties were enough to destroy the enemy's aviation. All the others were support actions for the ground troops."

"Since the destruction of the Egyptian bases by your planes, the Arabs and their Russian advisers have been thinking only of putting their planes, their radar, and their missiles underground."

"That's expensive, and it prevents their aircraft from acting swiftly. They have to bring their planes out from underground before they can use them! Maintenance is more difficult. Of course, we will have to find a way other than a surprise attack. We'll find it!

"The Egyptians now have 3,000 Soviet advisers, but I don't know whether they will succeed in teaching them how to fight in the sky—to bury themselves underground, surely."

"Will Israel have to give back the territories it is occupying?"

"It would still be necessary to negotiate with Israel. The Arabs refuse to recognize our existence. How is one to deal with a country that doesn't exist?

"It is more important for us to have the Sinai than to have fifty Mirage Vs. These new frontiers that we have conquered because the Arabs did not want to recognize our old frontiers —what a blessing for our air force! We can finally defend Tel Aviv and the cities on the coast. In the past, a few minutes would have been enough for the Egyptian bombers to be over our cities, not even giving us the time to intercept them. And then, too, we finally have enough space for our pilots to train in. The whole Sinai—it's great."

Motti extracts himself from his armchair and stands up. He points to the conquered territories on a map and suddenly smiles. He puts his finger on Mount Hermon, on the frontier of Syria and Lebanon.

"I was," he says, "in a helicopter with Moshe Dayan just over these mountains, the only ones where there is snow in this whole part of the East. The Syrians were fleeing in all directions, and we could take whatever we liked.

" 'What do you want for your aviators?' Dayan suddenly asked me.

"I showed him Mount Hermon.

" 'That mountain, so that they can go skiing.'

" 'It's yours.'

"*By radio, I immediately gave the order for a helicopter to put some men down there. Unfortunately, the peak (9,232 feet) was covered with clouds, and my commando group could take up a position only a little lower down. But we can now ski on Mount Hermon.*

"*Goodbye, monsieur; and above all don't forget my Mirages!*"

The Armored Cavalcade

Because of the narrowness of their territory, the Israeli armed forces lack room to maneuver on their own ground. Basically designed for a mobile war, the army can fight only on hostile territory. Although constituted as a defense force, it is condemned to invade. After rapidly assembling its troops, the vast majority of whom are reservists, it must act as did the cavalry in the Napoleonic wars: charging the enemy, routing him, pursuing him and exploiting victory on his rear. Israel has, in fact, only a cavalry—its armored brigades—and hardly any infantry except for a few shock troops like the commandos and paratroopers who are incorporated into the cavalry. Riding in jeeps and armed with 105 mm. recoilless rifles these "red berets" become reconnaissance troops. The rest of the time they advance with the tanks, as a spearhead or supporting them. They are usually in trucks and set down as near as possible to their objective. They attack swiftly, almost always by night, and then are picked up and returned to the brigade whose way they have just opened by blowing up a roadblock or an artillery post that was hampering the advance.

CONFRONTATION OF THE TANKS

June 1967 witnessed, in the Sinai desert, one of the greatest tank battles in military history. The Egyptian armed forces, deployed along the southern frontier of Israel, had more tanks than the German Panzer divisions that had fanned out across France or Marshal Rommel's Afrika Korps. On one side were seven Egyptian divisions (100,000 men) and 1,000 tanks, including 60 forty-six-ton Stalin IIIs, among the heaviest tanks in the world, 122 mm. guns and 200 mm. armor plating; and 100 thirty-six-ton T 55 tanks armed with 100 mm. guns and equipped with infrared radiation systems for night combat. The matériel included the most up-to-date output of the Russian war industry; experts proclaimed the T 55 one of the best tanks in the world, and some units of the Red Army had still not received it. The T 55s arrived in Egypt right off the assembly line. There were also 100 T 54s, 350 T 34s, 2,000 Su 100 tank destroyers (one of the most powerful ever known), 50 PT 76 amphibious tanks, a command tank armed with a 76 mm. gun, an infrared system, and, most important, extremely sophisticated radio equipment. But why an amphibious tank in the desert? People will puzzle over that for a long time, for in the entire Sinai there is not a single river, not even so much as a stream. In fact, in all Israel, except for the Jordan, there are hardly any rivers or streams. Finally, the Egyptians had some old Sherman tanks and a battalion of Centurions, dating from the time when Egypt's protectors were still British or American. All these forces were under a single command, that of General Murtaji.

The 4th Armored Division, Nasser's particular pride, the costly plaything that the Russians had given him, was organized like a large modern unit of the Red Army. It was composed of a brigade of 99 Stalin III tanks and 33 Su 100 tank destroyers, an infantry brigade supported by ten Su 100s, a regiment of field artillery with twenty-four 122 mm. guns, a group of 12 Katyusha rocket launchers, and an anti-aircraft unit of thirty-four guns.

The other six Egyptian divisions were composed of infantry supported by armored brigades, artillery regiments equipped with rocket launchers, and battalions with rapid-firing antitank weapons. Some of these weapons could fire bursts of ten hollow-loaded charges.

Facing this formidable armada, the Israelis mustered only three armored groups. There are no divisions in the Israeli army but only brigades, which can, furthermore, very easily be split into battalions and attached to this or that group. There is no rigidity in the arrangement of these big units, the composition of which is never settled but can vary at any moment in accordance with the necessities of combat.

All these units enjoy great autonomy; they can be self-sufficient for seventy-two hours, for they haul stores of fuel and ammunition behind them. The general in command of the southern front, General Yeshaya Gavish, supervised the operation more than he actually commanded it. As he knew his assistants very well there was no need for him to bury himself in details. He set the rhythm and the overall tactics and saw to logistics. The first of the groups, that of General Tal, had taken its position across from Khan Yunis. The second, under General Abraham Joffe, was made up entirely of reserves, including the officers, spread out between Rafah and Nitzana. General Arik Sharon's group was in position opposite Abu Aweigila farther south. In reserve were two brigades: one in the extreme south near Elath, facing El Kuntilla, the other opposite Gaza, north of the pocket.

It is difficult to say just how many tanks and men the Israelis had deployed: not more than 350–400 tanks and about 50,000 men. The Israeli soldiers were thus outnumbered two to one, their tanks three to one, and their weapons ten to one. We saw their tanks on parade in Jerusalem: old Shermans, Pattons, and British Centurions. Most are twenty years old. But, although these old carcasses remain outwardly the same, inside everything has been replaced. The Shermans have been rebuilt with more powerful motors; some of them, armed with heavy-caliber guns, have been turned into tank destroyers, and others retain only the motors and caterpillar tracks of the self-propelling artillery.

The Centurions have been equipped with a particular type of ammunition that worked wonders during this campaign: a shell perfected in the army workshops and in a sense a "secret weapon" but, once again, a makeshift affair. This projectile is propelled by an extremely powerful charge. Although it cannot penetrate the very thick armor of the Soviet tanks, its impact jars them so that the turrets jam, all the communications and sighting devices are knocked out, and the crew is banged up. It was with these shells that the Centurions rendered harmless the Stalin tanks, the T 54s, and the T 55s without destroying them.

The only modern tanks at the disposal of the Israeli brigades were French AMXs, which are fast and maneuverable, with light armor. Some of them were equipped with SS 10 and SS 11 rockets. One found these same rockets mounted on the trucks that served as tank destroyers. SS 10 and SS 11 rockets, guided by wires that could easily get caught in branches on the woody terrains of Europe, did not labor under the same handicap in the Sinai Deserts, on the Golan Heights, or along the Jordan. On the other hand, the Israeli artillery was very much inferior to that which the Russians had furnished the Egyptians. The whole Soviet doctrine of armor deployment is, as we have said, based on the massive concentration of artillery fire in a limited sector, where the tanks are to break through.

But the Egyptians do not possess a very aggressive spirit; they were all like Nasser, hoping to win the war without fighting it, and stayed dug in behind their solid fortifications, built according to Soviet plans. Nothing was really prepared for an offensive.

BATTLE OF THE DESERT

There are only three great east-west routes through the Sinai. All the armies that have wanted to cross it or to conquer it, from the tribes of Moses to Alexander, Napoleon, and in 1956 Moshe Dayan, have been forced to make use of them.

The first of these routes follows the coast: it runs from Gaza to El Qantara. It is defended near the Israeli frontier by the fortified perimeter around Rafah–El 'Arish. Throughout an area thirty-seven miles long and six miles wide were minefields, blockhouses, trenches, and underground depots for weapons, provisions, ammunition, and water tanks. To defend it there was a division of infantry, the 7th, and an armored brigade, equipped with 100 tanks, about one hundred 100 mm. and even 122 mm. guns, and heavy 120 mm. and 160 mm. mortars.

This line was going to be the toughest obstacle. El 'Arish is the administrative center of the Sinai and one of the biggest air bases, and Rafah is a great nexus of communications between the Sinai and the Gaza Strip. It was little General Tal, the tank man known as "Talik," who was responsible for this attack, on which the outcome of the war depended. He was given the best tank brigade and a brigade of paratroopers. The majority of his men were recruits or from the regular army. But he could not count on the support of the air force, which was occupied at the very moment of his attack in destroying the Egyptian air strips and bases. To his rear was the Egyptian 4th Armored Division, which it was also his job to annihilate.

The second route extends from Mitzana to Ismailia across desolate sands. It was defended by the fortified post of Abu Aweigila, about twelve miles from the frontier. The system of fortification there is the same as at Rafah and El 'Arish: three parallel lines of concrete entrenchments three miles long, which begin in the north with rocks and end in the south on the deadly sands and reputedly impossible dunes. In front of the first line was a minefield 250 yards wide. Three hundred yards behind it was the second line of trenches, and 750 meters farther back was the third line. These trenches were lined with concrete and linked by tunnels to weapons and ammunition storerooms. The base of operations was defended by the Egyptian 2nd Division, supported by very powerful artillery: 155 mm. guns, heavy mortars, and tanks of all types, which the Egyptians use most as first-line artillery.

General Sharon and his group were to take this position. Sharon had at his command a brigade of infantry transported by a motley automotive fleet—requisitions civilian buses, kibbutz trucks—an armored brigade reinforced by a battalion of Centurions, a reconnaissance formation, a detachment of engineers, a battalion of paratroopers, and six batteries of artillery and 120 mm. and 160 mm. mortars, which the Israelis were using for the first time.

Between Sharon and Tal was General Joffe's group, the most picturesque and disorderly, the one in which the average age was the highest and the beards the bushiest. Joffe himself, also a reserve officer, was fully in keeping with the rest of his unit thanks to his husky build, his thunderous voice, and his taste for whiskey. He is a great admirer of Hemingway and strives to emulate him.

Joffe was to take one of his armored brigades over a route that Cairo strategists considered impassable, in order to surprise the Egyptians from the rear south of El 'Arish near Bir Lafan. As soon as Sharon had taken Abu Aweigila, the second brigade was to pass him by and to fall on the Egyptian rear and circle Jebel Libni.

The third artery begins south of Elath on the shore of the Red Sea and runs to Suez by way of the Mitla Pass. In the middle of the Sinai, at Nakhl, this path, for it is no more than that, joins another coming from north or El Qusaima.

This route was blocked in the south, near Elath, by the "special operation" division of General Chazli, who was said to be one of the best Egyptian generals (even by the Israeli special services, which seems to grade Arab commanders like pupils in a class). He is a good-looking fellow, with broad shoulders and narrow hips, whom Radio Cairo called "our Rommel." He commanded four tank batallions, an infantry brigade, a batallion of commandos, and three batallions of artillery. As he was reputed to be the most aggressive of the Egyptian generals, his mission was to cut the Negev in two, to isolate Elath, and to link up with the Jordanians. North of Nakhl, the Egyptian 6th Division held the crossroads.

General Yariv's services had caused the Egyptians to believe that the Israeli army was going to attack in the south to break the blockade of Elath and the Strait of Tiran, the cause of the war. The brigade deployed opposite El Kuntilla busied itself there parading trucks under the noses of the Egyptians and Jordanians, driving down to Elath with their headlights on at night and back to their point of departure in darkness. Other trucks trailed branches and played at being tanks. By day, planes unloaded and reloaded the same trucks and jeeps.

We are going to try, by tracing the movements of the units through this gigantic tank battle and then by interviewing the generals who commanded them, to understand how the Israeli armored corps functions, what its particular characteristics are, how it so easily crushed a bigger army with more modern matériel and sheltered behind fortifications.

We shall question General Gavish, who commanded the entire front, then all the other generals: Tal, Sharon and Joffe.

OPERATION "RED SHEET"

The operation that was to end with the destruction of the whole Egyptian army was called "red sheet"—referring to the bedsheet of the wedding night, when the virgin is deflowered.

The numerical inferiority of the Israelis in men, tanks, and artillery was compensated for by their absolute mastery of the skies from the moment that the Arab air forces were pinned down.

But General Gavish, who supervised the whole operation, had foreseen that during the first days his tanks would not be able to count on an empty sky overhead. So they had been ordered to fight mostly by night and to be camouflaged in the daytime. Gavish instantly changed his plans, however, in the light of the new and reassuring tactical situation.

From the outset the Egyptians committed a number of mistakes. Although their lines of defense were solid and well organized, they were not continuous. Certain zones of approach to these positions were not defended because the chiefs of the Egyptian general staffs, who would not for anything in the world soil their elegant uniforms in the sands, judged them, a bit too hastily, to be "impassable" approach zones that Joffe's reserve noncoms advanced.

The Egyptians used tanks concentrated in fortified positions as artillery rather than as cavalry, which was contrary to Soviet teaching but suited the timorous temperament of the Egyptian generals. Finally, the Egyptian command had no mobile units in reserve, except for the famous 4th Armored Division, which was massed in the region of Bir Gifgafa. During the first days of the war, it waited to see what would happen instead of immediately coming to the aid of the positions in front of it, which were smashed or bypassed by the Israelis.

At 8 A.M., fifteen minutes after the air strike had begun, Operation Red Sheet was launched by the tanks. The objectives: to annihilate the Egyptian army of the Sinai in four days at most, before the United Nations could intervene.

General Tal advanced on El 'Arish and General Sharon on Abu Aweigila. General Joffe advanced between them on roads deemed impassable, to take the Egyptians from the rear.

Tal's Centurions and Pattons, supported toward the end of the first day by Fouga-Magisters—trainers converted into ground-support planes after being equipped with rockets and machine guns—broke through the defenses of Khan Yunis, leaving behind them the Egyptian and Palestinian forces, whom they had simply passed through. They continued on toward Rafah.

Many Israeli tanks were hit by antitank guns, but the mad armada kept advancing without worrying about its losses. The paratroopers charged the Egyptian positions in their jeeps, without protection, in order to force the Egyptian artillery to reveal its location. And so, Rafah was bypassed.

Before the entrenched post of El Jiradeh, the fiery Colonel Shmuel, who was commanding the attack, lost some time, for the Egyptians were resisting on all sides, but at 3:00 A.M. the following morning, the breakthrough to El 'Arish was finally made, thanks to the arrival of a batallion of reinforcements. The armies fought hand to hand in the light of rocket flares.

Tal's group had advanced sixty kilometers, destroyed four Egyptian brigades, and taken 100 pieces of artillery. But the paratroopers had paid dearly for this success. They suffered the heaviest losses. There is a rule, or rather a custom, according to which an ordinary unit retreats only after half its men have fallen—but the paratroopers never retreat.

Sharon had crossed the frontier at 8:30 A.M. and, in the midst of a sandstorm, had captured the first Egyptian positions before him. Surprise was in his favor, but there were no aircraft to aid him. He deployed before Abu Aweigila, which was defended by eighty-eight tanks, three artillery batallions, and a missile batallion. By the end of the day Abu Aweigila had been isolated and its outer defenses taken.

The storm subsided, and night fell. Two companies of paratroopers were airlifted by helicopter behind the enemy lines. Their mission: to muzzle the Egyptian guns, which could fire sixty miles farther than the Israeli cannons and so could not be neutralized by a counterbarrage. But, having landed too far from the objective, they had to cover ten miles on the run across the dunes. By midnight, after a fight carried out for the most part with hand grenades and knives, the operation was successful. The heavy 130 mm. guns were silent at last.

The first line was then smashed by the infantry, which attacked with grenades, cutting and blowing up the network of barbed wire with Bangalore torpedoes. The tanks penetrated the position. The Egyptians defended themselves more and more feebly. The second barrier to the Sinai had been over-turned.

Joffe's group made it across the dunes at the price of in-credible effort. One brigade passed Abu Aweigila, which had just been taken, and advanced toward Jebel Letni.

In the south, the Egyptian General Chazli, sensing that he was going to be cut off from Egypt, embarked on his retreat.

The audacious Tal divided his forces into two groups. One light column advanced toward Bir al-Romani and the Suez Canal, while the bulk of the forces made an oblique move-ment toward the south, where the strong post of Jebel Letni, one of the Sinai bases, stood. There they joined up with one of Joffe's brigades. The post was captured at nightfall. The road to Bir Gifgafa, where the Egyptian 4th Armored Division waited for it hardly knew what, was open.

Sharon meanwhile headed due south toward Nakhl, in order to cut off the retreat of General Chazli's independent force.

Gaza was taken by the brigade detached for the purpose, but the Palestinians fought courageously. The Egyptian gen-eral who was serving as Governor of Gaza surrendered the following day.

Moshe Dayan sent this message to all his unit commanders: "Advance; we don't have much time left. The Security Coun-cil is getting ready, in fact, to order the cease-fire."

On Wednesday came a great race between the Israeli tanks, which were advancing everywhere, and the Egyptians, who were withdrawing toward Suez. "The day before, the Sinai was still a battleground; that day, it was to become a cemetery" (Yves Cuau, *Israël attaque*, Paris: Laffont). Tal's first column reached the Suez near El Qantara, but had to withdraw twenty-five miles "for political reasons," while the bulk of his forces came in contact with the Egyptian 4th Ar-mored Division, the elite unit, the most heavily armed unit in the whole Middle East.

Badly cut up and pounded by the air force, the 4th Division was still resisting when night fell. At 3:00 A.M. Nasser sent all his reserves—about 100 T 55 tanks, the most recent models, equipped for night combat—to help the 4th break out of the Israeli encirclement. To stop them there were AMXs, supported at the end by a company of Centurions.

The Joffe group, after taking Bir Hassina, attempted to close the Mitla Pass, through which the remnants of the Egyptian army would have to pass in order to reach the canal. The Egyptian and Israeli tanks struggled to outdistance each other and sometimes rolled along side by side without even exchanging fire.

Nine Israeli tanks were the first to reach the Mitla Pass—twelve miles boxed in by dunes and rocks. Planes chased the game toward them. It was a massacre. The nine tanks held out all night. Sharon's group captured a brigade of Stalin tanks, which their crews had abandoned in perfect working condition and fully stocked with gasoline and ammunition. The Egyptian general commanding them had tried to flee in a half-track. When taken prisoner, his one concern was for the fine leather suitcases that he had lost. Sharon reached Nakhl at the same time as the first elements of Egyptian Rommel Chazli's special force: Fifty Egyptian tanks, two regiments of artillery, and 800 vehicles were destroyed. General Chazli fled on foot. He swam across the Canal after having wandered for several weeks in the desert. If it was not a military victory, it was at least an athletic feat.

The Egyptian army was destroyed, with all its matériel. Sharm el-Sheikh, which guards the Strait of Tiran, was abandoned without a fight. Israeli paratroopers and marines occupied it.

On Thursday all the Israeli troops fanned out toward the Canal. El Qantara was seized after a battle in which Colonel Rafoul's paratroopers, mounted on top of their jeeps and armed with 105 mm. guns, destroyed T 55 tanks, which even the Pattons had not been able to do.

The soldiers of three armored groups had not slept for four

days. They had lost 280 men killed and 800 wounded. It is impossible to estimate the Egyptian losses in men—around 20,000. Many soldiers lost their way and died of thirst in the desert, which was transformed into a charnel house of corpses and burnt-out tanks, which stank unbearably. The battle of Sinai had lasted four days. On June 4 Colonel Nasser had declared: "We are more aflame than live coals as we wait to do battle against Israel. This battle will demonstrate to all the world who the Arabs are and what Israel is."

That has been demonstrated.

GENERAL GAVISH SPEAKS

General Yeshaya Gavish, whom everyone calls by his nickname Chaike, is a calm, good-humored giant, who seems very much at ease with himself. He loves war and the army and doesn't try to hide it. At eighteen, while still a student in an agricultural institute, he enlisted in the Palmach and busied himself organizing clandestine immigration, which put him in the bad books of the British, who arrested him in June 1946 in the "Black Sabbath" roundup. Although badly wounded, he finished the 1948–1949 campaign with the rank of battalion commander.

From 1958 to 1960 he studied at the War College in Paris and in 1963 he became the army's training chief. At that time the Egyptians and Syrians had just adopted Soviet tactics. Chaike decided that he would, as a consequence, have to modify the organization and, in particular, the training of the army, and especially of the tank corps.

In 1966 he took command of the southern sector. He already knew then that it would be in the Sinai once again that renewed fighting would have to take place.

General Gavish receives me in the office of the former military governor of Gaza, the Egyptian General Munam Abdul Husaini. In the anteroom is a big photograph of Mecca: The

Israelis have kept it. Gavish has just returned from a tour through the desert, and his face is burned by the sun and wind.

I ask him the reasons for the victory of the Israeli tanks in the Sinai, seeing that they were less numerous and less well armed than the Egyptian tanks were.

"The reasons for our victory? I know at least ten. It is quite true that we were weaker. As against 950 Egyptian tanks— T 54s, T 55s, Centurions, Stalins, Su 100s—we were able to line up only 450 tanks, half of which were of roughly the same type and half much lighter than those of the Egyptians.

Our most powerful guns, the 155 mms., had a range of only ten miles, whereas the Soviet 130 mm. guns had a range of fifteen miles. The Egyptians had 1,000 artillery pieces at their disposal. As for us, well, we were completely out of it.

"But let me go back to my reasons.

"Here's the first: The Egyptians didn't know how to use tanks as mobile armored units. They looked upon them simply as artillery. They made the same mistake that the French made in 1940 when the latter spread their 4,000 tanks all along the frontiers. The Germans, with 2,500 tanks grouped in armored divisions, broke through wherever they chose. In a tank war concentration equals victory. We concentrated our three armored groups within a width of less than thirty miles, while the Egyptians deployed theirs throughout the entire Sinai.

"Second reason: It is infinitely more difficult for an officer to command mobile armored units than a stationary army sheltered behind fortifications. Unlike the Egyptians, we chose movement. We trained our tank men under the same conditions as those they would encounter in the war for which we were preparing. We made as many as 250 tanks at a time take part in maneuvers with live ammunition. We selected practice terrains similar to those on which our tanks would have to fight. In fact, they were a lot more than just maneuvers. The physical conditions of that training were as *rough, if not rougher, than those of the actual war—the lack of sleep, for example. Our men were thus not thrown off by the efforts we asked of them in June 1967.*

The Egyptian general-staff officers went through the same exercises, but only on maps and with piles of sand: the Kriegspiel [war game]. So they were incapable of commanding as quickly and effectively as our officers on the actual field of battle.

"The third reason: Because of the political implications of the war, we were constrained to act very quickly, and the enemy never had time to react with the same speed.

"If everybody waged war as it is described in the manuals, nobody would win. We acted against all the rules the Egyptians knew. Taken by surprise, they had no idea how to react. We didn't follow any specific theory of warfare: We innovated as we went along. An instructor in an English military school asked me: 'How do you manage to have tank drivers who don't sleep for four days? What's the mystery? Do you change your crews?'

"I answered that there is no mystery to it, that we had been training our crews for a long time not to sleep for four successive nights in anticipation of a very fast war. For we had to conduct a rapid war with the Arabs. We had to beat them without losing speed. The Arabs and, in particular, the Egyptians, neither think nor react very quickly. They have to reflect a long time. Men like the Arabs, who ruminate over their beads, have all the time in the world before them. Not us.

"The fourth reason: To maintain our impact, we never slowed our advance. Normally, once our tanks had arrived at El 'Arish, we would have had to pause—which would have enabled the Egyptians to reinforce their second line of defense. But we didn't respect at any time the tactical theories that the Russians had drummed into their protégés. Our tanks refueled on the move, our men swallowed dog biscuits.

"The fifth reason: Without altering the disposition of our

forces before attacking, we always isolated the battlefield. We blocked escape routes to prevent the enemy from either fleeing or receiving reinforcements.

"The sixth reason: We took our tanks across country that was theoretically impassable, as Hannibal had done in the Alps and the Germans in the Ardennes. We thrust an armored brigade into dunes that were said to be uncrossable. The tanks made it, but the supply vehicles couldn't follow. So we parachuted gasoline and ammunitions to the tanks. We preferred to take this risk rather than to be unable to isolate the battlefield.

"The seventh reason: Our logistics. Each unit had to have always with it, and to replenish continually, seventy-two hours' worth of ammunition, provisions, and gasoline. The gasoline followed the armored groups, taking the risks, of course, that are involved in having fuel trucks next to tanks.

"The eighth reason: Our aerial superiority. The sky was empty, and all our aircraft could support us on the ground, directly or indirectly. We were by no means certain of having this mastery of the skies. We were trained to camouflage our vehicles by day and to fight by night. Don't forget that for three weeks our three armored groups had been perfectly camouflaged on an absolutely flat desert.

"The ninth reason: The quality and swiftness of our intelligence. To know how the enemy is arrayed on his first line of defense is relatively easy; it's a matter of operational intelligence—patrols, aerial photos, and the like. But for this intelligence to reach you progressively as the battle is going on, in such a way that you can change your plans and tactics on the spot at any moment, is infinitely more difficult. Intelligence must be instantly translated into battle plans. The Egyptians showed themselves incapable of doing this.

"We never stopped doing it.

"We also had at our disposal an extremely rapid network of telecommunications.

"The tenth reason: We were continuously ready to change

our plans and even to abandon the tactics that we had previously employed. The war was, for us, constant improvisation, not the application of rules. We learned, after the first phase of the battle, that the entire Egyptian army was preparing to retreat to a second line of fortifications, of which we knew nothing.

"In one hour we changed all our battle plans. Our mission was not to conquer the Sinai but to annihilate the Egyptian army. So we took the risk: It was no longer a question of isolating the battlefields or of fighting against forces whose numbers were known. We advanced without giving a thought to anything else. It was a marathon race. We often left behind us enemy units that had not been destroyed and that might have cut off our return, but we went forward.

"We had to improvise, to take advantage of the terrain as it came; for example, we discovered at the Mitla Pass that about ten well-placed tanks could demolish 150 tanks that attempted all through one night to force the position.

"We had one preoccupation: to keep the enemy from having time to reorganize.

"These, I think, were the principal reasons for our victory. I have, of course, forgotten the main one: the quality of the Israeli soldier."

GENERAL TAL SPEAKS

General Tal, known as Talik, lord of the Sinai, who commanded the 1st Armored Group, the one that had to force the posts of El 'Arish and Khan Yunis, is a short, brown-haired man with a comic look, perhaps because of his slightly turned-up nose. Born in 1924 in upper Galilee, he enlisted at eighteen and served with the British army in the Italian campaign. In 1948 he took part in the battle of Jerusalem, went to Czechoslovakia to buy weapons, and returned to Jerusalem, where he put in two years of study at the university (philosophy and political science). Then he went back into the army.

It was decided to turn this foot soldier into the leading tank man. Ten years later he had become the great specialist of the tank force. In 1964 he was appointed director of the armored cavalry. Upon leaving the army he hopes to become a teacher after having worn the uniform for twenty-seven years.

General Tal receives me in Tank House. Below, in a big hall, they are celebrating the marriage of some soldier or tank officer. Only Coca-Cola and orange soda, very Jewish beverages, are being served, but there are very pretty flowers on the tablecloths.

I ask him the same question that I asked Gavish, "How did you win, even though your tanks were older, less heavily armored, and slower than those of the Egyptians?"

He goes off to answer a ringing telephone, then returns:

"For both political and economic reasons, we weren't able to procure the tanks we needed. We had to fall back on the old Shermans which, when modernized—with a more powerful engine and another gun—nevertheless demolished, for example, the Jordanian Pattons.

"The only modern item we received was the French AMX light tank. Yet twenty of these light tanks knocked out, in one battle, fifty Soviet heavy tanks. Why? Because we know how to fight at night, which the Egyptians do not know, and because our men aim better and fire at closer range.

"Our crews know how to use all kinds of tanks, all kinds of guns, all kinds of ammunition. Jordanian tanks, Centurions captured during the war, were used in April of this year against the same Jordanians, at Kuraiyima. Our victory was owing particularly to the quality of our men. Our tank crews have a very thorough knowledge of their job. They are actually expert mechanics, who can repair their vehicles even in the field.

"And then, we are more alone than any other people in the world. One of my brigade commanders told his men before

the battle, 'If we don't win, we won't know where to go or whom to turn to.'

"A people's destiny shapes its conduct, and destiny has made us a nation of warriors. Our tank crews, condemned to be courageous, fought with extraordinary courage. Wounded soldiers continued to fight until the moment they died. Burning tanks continued to fire. Our tanks charged as the cavalry did in olden times. They could not retreat: Where was there to retreat to? They could not lose without condemning their wives and children to death."

I ask "Talik" what, in his opinion, would be the ideal tank for the Israeli army?

"One that I will build myself, from my own design, fit for a terrain and a kind of warfare that I know well. Unfortunately, we are still a long way from being able to manufacture our own tanks. Economically, it's impossible. Too bad!"

"How does one become a general in Israel?"

"Natural selection!"

COLONEL SHMUEL SPEAKS

One of the top specialists of the Israeli army is Colonel Shmuel, who commands the advance units of Tal's group, stationing himself, of course, out in front with the reconnaissance jeeps.

A native of Lithuania who came to Israel at the age of three, he followed a course of rabbinical studies in a yeshiva, from which he went directly into the Haganah. Today, at thirty-eight, he is fiercely atheistic. His face is round, his hair short.

At Quneitra, in his command post, he is seated on a cot and I on a footstool; he insists that I toss off several glasses of Israeli vodka, which is not of the best quality.

In his turn, he gives me reasons for the superiority of the Israelis over the Egyptians during the Sinai campaign: "It *depended first and foremost on the transmission and execu-tion of orders. Because the brigade commander was out in front and commanded directly, he won out every time over his Egyptian counterpart, who was always in the rear.*

"Units like the brigade are organized in such a flexible way that they can split up and reform without the slightest difficulty. . . .

"Tanks that were hit and immobilized nevertheless con-tinued to fire. At Rafah, for instance, two Pattons hit by the fire of T 34s burst into flames. Even so, they destroyed the T 34s, and the crews did not get out of the tanks until their ammunition exploded. They apologized for losing the tanks.

"At Khan Yunis, the crew of a Centurion whose engine had been hit took up rifles and hand grenades, went off to clean out some enemy trenches, came back, repaired their engine, and took off again.

"A wounded or dead man is never abandoned. This abso-lute rule gives the men who fight more confidence.

"Every soldier can, at any moment, have his orders ex-plained to him, ask any of his officers what is going on, why he is where he is, or what they are going to do or try to do the next day. He has the right to be kept informed about how the battle is going.

"We never cheat on results. We tell the truth, however painful it may be at times. Our intelligence reports are con-sequently always accurate, no matter how vanity is damaged.

"Finally, we had remarkable crews of mechanics, who managed to repair and even change the engine of a tank in the middle of a battle."

To all these excellent reasons, we must not forget to add the gift for "tinkering," which the Israeli people possess to a very high degree. One example:

In the course of this Six-Day War, the Israelis tried out a quick method of distributing fuel. Mounted on requisitioned civilian trucks were rubber containers holding thousands of liters, each equipped with several tubes, which serviced a number of tanks simultaneously. . . . The only area in which the needs outran preparations was that of water. The Israeli army had not provided for a sufficient number of water trucks. To dispatch water to where it was needed milk delivery tanks had to be requisitioned in the cities and towns. (Ben Elissar and Schiff, *La guerre*)

GENERAL SHARON SPEAKS

General Ariel Sharon (but with the Israeli soldiers' mania for hanging diminutives on their generals, he is called Arik) was born in 1928 in a kibbutz. He enlisted in the Haganah, was twice wounded, and took part in the encirclement of the Egyptian army at Faluja. Among the Egyptian officers was a certain Gamal Abdel Nasser, who was to brood for a long time over his rage at having been beaten by a gang of ragged soldiers without uniforms, no two of whom had the same make of rifle. Arik Sharon next studied at the University of Jerusalem. He earned a law degree and was admitted to the bar. But he missed the army. He went back to it and created Special Force 101. This commando unit subsequently conducted most of the organized reprisal raids outside the Israeli frontiers. In the course of one of these raids Sharon was wounded again. In 1956 he commanded a brigade of paratroopers in the Sinai, and, after taking part in the capture of El Kuntilla and Nakhl, he made for the famous Mitla Pass and blocked it to keep the Egyptians from retreating.

At forty, General Sharon has light-colored eyes—the eyes of a Norseman—and a smiling face that sometimes tightens and grows hard. On his head is the red beret of the French paratroopers, of a garnet red different from that of the Israeli "paras." A French officer who accompanied him in the Sinai gave it to him in recognition for his having fought so well and thereby honored all paratroopers, no matter to what nations they belong.

Yaël Dayan, the daughter of Moshe Dayan, who was at-

tached as a lieutenant to General Sharon's staff during the
Six-Day War, describes him as follows:

Handsome face, laughing eyes, straight nose, a body perhaps a
bit heavy but very much at ease in campaign clothes. . . . Despite
his youthful appearance, his hair is silvered; it is wavy and hides
a very high forehead. His trailer (which served as his command
post) was quite impersonal and as simple as it could be. Two
wooden benches served as a bed at night. On the big table one
sometimes ate and sometimes worked. Arik's personal effects
fitted into a rucksack smaller than mine. . . .
Arik's voiced changed when he spoke to Danny [Colonel Danny
Mat], commander of the paratroopers. He had commanded them
himself. They were his boys; he knew them all by their first
names. In a certain sense, he gave the impression of talking to
a brother to whom he had confided a difficult task. (Yaël Dayan,
Lieutenant au Sinaï, Paris: Laffont)

*We find him to be just like that when we talk to him about
the paratroopers. He is the real creator of that corps. At
present, Arik is responsible for the entire training of the
Israeli army, and to see the man in his beret is to grasp at
once the particular orientation he gives to it.*

*"I love the army," General Sharon tells me. "I have held
every rank from platoon leader to general. I lived through a
crucial moment in the history of the Israeli army, when, with
men from all sorts of more or less clandestine organizations
and officers from the British army or the Palmach, it transformed itself into a real body of troops.*

*"But even today the only generals who hold commands
come from the Palmach. In the Palmach you became an officer because you had it in you and not because you had taken
such and such training. We were all civilians. Our training
never stopped. We prepared ourselves for the war of 1948 in
the underground and through acts of sabotage, for that of
1956 and the Six-Day War by commando activities in the
neighboring Arab countries. They continued without letup
since 1962."*

I ask the general: "This army, then, began with commandos. In the commandos the number of officers is greater than in any other group. Is that why so many officers are killed in Israel?"

"We have no more officers in one of our companies than, for example, the Americans. But we give them a special training that makes the captain the best soldier in the company. That soldier, then, advances at the head of his troops—and it's the same at all levels of command. Besides, it's infinitely easier to command when you're ahead of your men, especially in the kind of tank battles that took place in the Sinai.

"The war began on Monday morning. I left my headquarters Monday evening and didn't get back to it until Friday. My staff officers scattered among all the brigades. I found myself up ahead, in front, and thus I was able to transmit my orders on the basis of what I could see. At the same time I had, in each unit, men with whom I was accustomed to work, who knew how to keep me informed and who understood my orders.

"The Egyptian generals were never at the head of their men. And what delays! Speed is the main thing in this kind of war. Let's take an example: Two armored brigades, one Israeli, one Egyptian, are face to face. At the head of the Israeli brigade is its commanding officer; he assesses the situation, immediately gives orders, and deploys his tanks. At the head of the Egyptian brigade is some captain or commander who reports his situation to the general's field headquarters, which is always in the rear. Certain details of this report are already out of date. The reaction, which ought to be instantaneous, takes several minutes. When orders finally arrive at the front, garbled still further by all those who have transmitted them and understood them imperfectly, the situation has completely changed. We Israelis, not having these delays in transmission and not having wasted time in reflection, are already in place for battle while the Egyptians are executing their first movements.

"*Everything depends on speed, and speed can be attained only through clear, direct orders given by an officer who is not only right there on the field of battle but with the reconnaissance units.*

"*Speed, therefore youth. And that is why, with us, generals age so quickly and have to be replaced so soon, because in their forties they have to live constantly at the insane tempo of youths of twenty.*"

"*To what do you attribute your victory, General? To the poor quality of the Egyptian army?*"

"*The Egyptian soldier is no worse than any other, but like his officer he is quite without initiative, and, above all, he is very slow. His mind is slow, and his legs are heavy. The Egyptians, whether officers or privates, have hardly changed at all since the war of 1956. By contrast, ours have developed a great deal—because we wanted them to. Faced with that army, which refuses to change and which lacks imagination, it immediately occurred to us to use the least conventional and predictable tactics. We know that the Egyptian command, having no initiative and no imagination at any level, will be undone by anything unforeseen. In actual fact, victory always depends on the training of the soldier. The Egyptian soldier's training has not been changed at all. We Jews start with a totally different concept of warfare. For us, winning a battle is not a matter of taking a particular terrain, a mountain, a plain, a desert, or even a city. It is a matter of destroying the enemy army. We can lose battles while advancing all the way to Cairo and Damascus if we have not destroyed the enemy battle corps, particularly if we have massive casualties. We are not very numerous, and we cannot afford too many deaths. With each death, we lose our own blood. For the Egyptians, and the Arabs in general, blood doesn't count. They are 70 million, and we are 2 million.*

"*Look here: If I had to give you one reason for our victory, I would say that it was rooted in the profound and critical studies we ourselves make, at all levels, after each battle, each engagement, each commando raid. We draft regular books in each instance; they are then compiled by the army's historical services. Everything is studied, down to the smallest detail, after close interrogation of the participants. These reports somehow sum up the debate—in other countries it would be called self-criticism—that the chief of staff himself presides over immediately after the operation, in the presence of all the participants. In this way it happens that, starting from a single study of a foiled raid, we end up collectively working out a new tactic. It is twenty years now that we have been operating this way. You must understand that our science is founded on experience and that experience is costly, since we pay in blood every time. We insist on making maximum use of it.*

"But our victory depended on neither matériel nor on tactics nor on the officers who made use of the first or perfected the second—but on the Israeli soldier, distinguished, above all, by his training as a paratrooper."

MOBILIZATION BY TRANSISTOR

One of the essential qualities of the Israeli army is the rapidity of its mobilization. It is an army of reserves (60,000 men in the active, or regular, army, and 240,000 in the reserves). For the air force, hardly any problems of mobilization exist, as the majority of the pilots belong to the regular army and are on a perpetual state of alert. It is quite different with the tank corps.

The Israeli high command has endeavored, through intensive training and frequent alerts, to reduce to a maximum of twenty-four hours the time that elapses between the moment when a tank reservist is called to service by radio or telephone and the moment when he is in his vehicle on the battlefield, ready to engage the enemy.

The reservist always has ready his combat uniform and

shoes, but not his weapons. Officers keep their pistols, however. The radio broadcasts a code message, usually borrowed
from the Bible, to summon this or that unit: Rose of Sharon,
for example, is the code order to a particular group of reserves to go at once and by whatever means to a certain point
in the Negev or Galilee, most often the Negev. (The instant
the political situation starts to deteriorate all Israelis live
with one ear glued to their transistors, which they take with
them wherever they go.) Or some unit member may summon
others by telephone or pick them up at their homes. The
Israeli high command has always seen to it that the reserves
of a given unit live in the same district of a city, in the same
village or the same kibbutz, which simplifies the methods of
mobilization. From the moment that mobilization is ordered,
private cars no longer exist. Everything belongs to Israel.
Men pile into any old vehicle, a friend's car, for example, or
perhaps a taxi, which they have no need to requisition as the
driver volunteers to go with them. By truck, bus, and car
everybody takes off in all directions for the bases. In a few
hours, big cities like Tel Aviv are completely empty, and the
stylish sidewalk cafés of Dizengoff Circle are deserted. If the
Israeli army has a real secret, it is in those bases, where all
the matériel needed to equip an armored brigade, for example, is stored. Each reserve soldier finds, in a bin with his
name on it, his perfectly maintained weapons, his reserve
provisions, his first-aid kit, his gear, his radio helmet, and so
on. The moment he is ready he makes for a broad space
where the tanks, which have just been brought out of their
shelters, are waiting. These tanks are in perfect working condition, loaded with gasoline and ammunition. The engines
are running; all the soldier has to do is jump in and drive off.
On board there is an envelope containing maps and showing
the points where the tanks will regroup. One of the main activities of the career army is the maintenance of matériel,
which must be ready for use by the reserves at any moment.
A core of specialists exists; it is joined in the first hours of

mobilization by units of the "spearhead reserve." These men are reserves who have only just left the active army and are consequently still at the peak of training. They are the first to be called and must get to these depots within a few hours to help ready all the stored matériel for service.

These storage bases remain one of the Israeli army's most vulnerable points. If they were bombed, the Tsahal would be deprived of much of its potential. So they are scattered throughout the entire Negev desert and extremely well hidden. It has been said that during the three weeks before the Six-Day War immense fleets of private cars were to be seen in the middle of the desert, surrounding the Israeli brigades that were forming up.

GENERAL JOFFE SPEAKS

Abraham Joffe is the archetype of those reserve generals whose influence remains great in the inner circles of the army even after they have left it—and outside the army because of the civilian functions they fulfill. In May 1967, a few days before the state of alert was proclaimed, Joffe was in the Camarque in southern France, where he had gone to study the organization of the regional park that was to be created there.

This outspoken, corpulent giant began, before being charged with the protection of nature, by being himself a great destroyer. He hunted passionately, as he did everything else, and began to poach, "which was not permitted," as one of his friends told me. Denounced and arrested, he was brought before a tribunal and sentenced to a rather stiff penalty. He swore to turn over a new leaf—and so the wolf became a shepherd. At the present time there is in all Israel no better defender of the country's flora and fauna. His conversion resulted in his being appointed director of the national parks of Israel.

Abraham Joffe was born in 1913 in upper Galilee. At sixteen, he joined the Haganah and in 1940 the British army, in which he became a lieutenant. He fought in the Middle East and got to know Leclerc and Montgomery. During the war of independence, he was the colonel in command of the celebrated Golani Brigade. We find him again, in 1958, at the head of the southern military region; he became a general and, in 1962, the commanding officer of the northern military region. In 1964 he retired. He was recalled to active duty to command one of the three tank groups in the Sinai.

I seek him out in a shabby office, at the very top of a gray-cement building of an ugliness surprising even in that quarter of Tel Aviv, which is filled with grim piles. On the walls are photographs of Flemish roses, birds in flight, and wild animals, most of them clipped from magazines. Here I am in the Office of National Parks. It is obvious at once that its director is not in this retreat very often but is usually on the move around Israel. General Joffe, his shirt open across his imposing belly, his nose thrust toward me, his eyes sharp, demands, "Well then?"

"General, you have the reputation of being a trainer of men who is dynamic, sometimes violent."

"Go on, say it: 'as an old bastard.'"

"Now I find you a protector of nature. How did you get into this?"

"It's not very complicated. When I left the army, I looked for a job that would allow me to spend as much time as possible away from an office, preferably in the open air, and to have as few contacts as possible with those shits in the Histadrut (The General Confederation of Israeli Workers, which encompasses half the population of the country). Most of my comrades, colonels or generals like myself, often accept, on their retirement, directorships of big civilian enterprises. And then stupidities begin with the Histadrut. Long live the wide open spaces, monsieur, the stags, the hinds, the birds! Let's protect them."

The ogre does not seem to me as repentant as he means to sound. When I speak of game, his eyes glisten.

I ask him: "During the Six-Day War, you were in command of the biggest reserve unit of all. What do you think of those reserves?"

"The greatest. To execute the mission that was entrusted to me—to cross the dunes—I had to have men who were solid, quick, tough, and resourceful. The reserves are very quick, better than my regular soldiers, who are still kids. My soldiers were between twenty-two and thirty-five, my officers sometimes forty. At that age, they understand very well what they have to do and how to go about doing it. The reservists all get together every year for a given period; they live in the same area or the same town, and sometimes they are neighbors. All this creates strong ties of friendship and solidarity and makes for a solid troop. We paid particular attention to the speed of mobilizing the reserves. Let's take the example of a unit of Centurions under my command. From the moment when the reserves who manned the tanks were summoned by radio to the moment when the tanks left and grouped in units ready for combat, less than forty-eight hours went by.

"In case of mobilization, each reserve soldier knows exactly where he must go and which tank he must climb into. He also knows that he will find his tank is in perfect working condition and that all the machinery will have been scrupulously inspected. We have obtained these results through an unremitting and very hard training of our reserves, a training that is harder than war itself. This has cost us dear. We have smashed up matériel. But the proof that this system works is that we won."

"And why did you win?"

"The Egyptians of the armored units did not understand mobile warfare. Their tanks could fire rapidly and, if necessary, execute a simple circling maneuver. But their officers panicked when it was a question of executing more complex

maneuvers, when it was necessary to drive at night, for ex-
ample, or to change formation. That was true at all levels."

"And now that the war is over?"

Joffe slaps the table. "The war is not over, since the Arabs
still constantly proclaim, on their lousy radio, that they want
to erase Israel from the world map. But with the new terri-
tories we now hold, they can wait. So I would violently op-
pose any maneuver which, on the pretext of signing a peace
treaty that would not be honored, would lead us to give up
the conquered territories. We keep them; that's all there is to
it. It's up to us to find a solution to the problem of the
Palestinian refugees: perhaps a Palestinian confederation.
It will be a long and difficult task. But we will discover the
solution—in an empirical way, by getting to know the Pales-
tinians better and arriving at an understanding with them."

I leave General Joffe, with his powerful bulk completely
dominating his little scholar's office, surrounded by those
wild beasts and brightly colored birds that one finds in pic-
ture books.

The Paratroopers
Before the Wailing Wall

"I swear and pledge on my honor to keep faith with Israel, with its laws and with its leaders, to accept unconditionally and without argument the discipline of the Defense Forces of Israel, to obey all orders that are given to me by my officers, to consecrate all my strength, even to give my life, for the defense of the country and for the freedom of Israel."

The text of this oath, which was that of the clandestine Haganah, is read aloud by a young officer. After him each soldier simply repeats, "I swear it." Then, standing at attention, he receives from the hand of the sergeant who will be his instructor, starting the next day, a rifle and a Bible. The ceremony takes place in the flickering light of flames burning in tin cans filled with gasoline-soaked packing. Before us is the Wailing Wall, with its cyclopean stone blocks.

THE OATH

All new recruits to the tank corps take their oath on the height of the citadel of Masada after a three-day march; the recruits of the women's army before the burned-out skeletons of a convoy that tried to force the Jerusalem road in 1948; those of the air force on Mount Herzl among trees as numerous as the millions of Jews killed in concentration camps. The infantry soldiers take their oath on Hill 113 near Ashquelon which was conquered after heavy losses during the war of independence and the supply units at Modiin, the homeland of the Maccabees. The paratroopers, by taking the Old City of Jerusalem in hand-to-hand combat so as not to destroy the holy places, have won the glorious privilege of taking theirs before Israel's most sacred spot, this massive wall, the last vestige of the Temple of Solomon.

The future paratroopers—they were called to the colors only a week ago—first marched twenty-five miles. They started at dawn and arrived only at nightfall under the walls of Jerusalem. They still do not have the right to bear weapons and carry only knapsacks and uniform gear. They are not holy cavaliers, although it is with that old Crusaders' ritual that the ceremony of the oath seems to be connected. Yet, how angrily the Israelis reject every comparison with the knights of the Crusades—who stayed in the Holy Land only for one century!

The recruits are massed in front of a little platform surrounded by a few benches for their parents and friends. Behind them rises the Wall, before which members of all the Hebrew sects dance and wail: Hasidim, who seem to be dancing a surrealistic ballet in their long black gowns; Orthodox Jews from the depths of Russia, Poland, or Rumania, miraculously escaped from the Nazi death camps, the pogroms of the Czar's Cossacks, and Stalin's G.P.U. Among them there are even some American Jews, who are suddenly and fanatically rediscovering the sacred swaying movements and who swing their fat bellies in cadence under the mocking eyes of the lean Hasidim, who look like professional dancers compared to them.

All these Jews consider the presence of soldiers before the Wall a sacrilege. They intend to protest in their own way, by yelling louder and louder to drown out the speeches and songs that follow the oath.

The floodlights illuminating the Wall dim, as innumerable

flames spring up to form the Israeli paratroopers' insignia. The rabbi of the army, bearded and tightly corseted in his close-fitting uniform, mounts the dais. Speaking into a microphone, he launches into a rather long address, in the course of which he frequently quotes the Bible, which, it seems to me, has the effect of heightening the rage of the "old Jews," for their cries redouble. Then Colonel Danny Mat speaks in his turn. A neighbor translates his speech for me.

Colonel Mat is a kind of bearded giant with a lean body, a "modern" body, with a biblical head on top. He led the brigade of paratroopers attached to General Sharon's command during the Six-Day War. With the same brigade he later attacked the al-Fatah bases in the little Jordanian town of Kuraiyima. Danny Mat attended the War College in France with Bigeard, whom he resembles in manner—his way of walking, and handling himself with his men, charming them and overwhelming them at the same time. He is one of the few officers in the Israeli army with a family tradition of command; his father was a career officer in the armies of the old Austro-Hungarian Empire.

"Paratroopers:

"A year ago, I would have spoken to you of peace, for the war had just ended. Many of our men had died in conquering this city and this Wall, and we thought only of peace."

He turns in irritation toward the noisy black figures, leftovers of a past far from pleasing to an Israeli soldier, who are dancing about over there to the rear, against the Wall. They are still wearing side curls, as in the ghettos of Poland and are still behaving as if Israel does not exist, as if the army has not taken up again, after the dark ages of the Diaspora, the glorious military tradition of the judges of David and the Maccabees. He pauses a few moments, then continues. The paratroopers, who listened to the rabbi in boredom, follow Mat with keen interest.

"I would then have spoken to you of peace. But not today. Once again you are going to experience fear, suffering, blood, and tears. We must not allow ourselves any illusions; we shall have war again, and again we shall have to win in order not to be obliterated. So this is what I wish for you: a very hard, very painful training. I wish you sweat, thirst, and exhaustion.

"Never forget that you are the shield and the lance of Israel, and that without you our country and our hope would cease to exist. So long."

Then, the Israeli national anthem is sung; it sounds like a very slow hymn, and all the soldiers take it up in chorus. This time their voices drown the cries of the "old Jews." These young soldiers are the future of Israel. Not a single one of them has the hooked nose, the bent back, the waxy pallor of the ghetto Jews; all are tanned and lean and hold their heads high. (Arthur Koestler once suggested that, if Scandinavians were stuck in a ghetto for three generations and forced to marry only among themselves, then they, too, would have crooked noses, bent backs, and the pale skins.) With the training they are going to undergo, one of the toughest in the world, they will be changed again into remarkable and highly dangerous warriors. Those other people, over there by the Wall, hopping about like jumping-jacks on strings manipulated by God knows who, belong to the past. But in handing the young soldiers Bibles along with their rifles the army chiefs seek to remind them that they are supposed to defend, not only a country, but also a religion and a tradition in whose name the miracle of the return to the promised land was accomplished.

A little later I find Colonel Mat, still wearing a red beret, standing before the Wall, next to the rabbi of the army and surrounded by black gowns. He is holding a prayer book in his hands, but he is not reading.

I ask him, "Are you a practicing Jew?"

"No."

"Why are you here?"

"To show these people here who wanted to drown out the oath that the Wailing Wall belongs to us too. Although it is part of their religion, it belongs to our history. We are the ones who reconquered it; it was not by their prayers that we took it but by our blood."

"What does the Bible mean to you?"

"A history book, the book of our history."

"Do you think that Israel will have to fight another war?"

"Yes."

"Do you love war?"

"No, but I love my paratroopers. I know I am going to have to leave them some day. I'm over forty. I'm going to have a very hard time doing it."

"How important are the paratroopers in Israel?"

"They are the ones who have left their stamp on the army. Nowadays, nobody can be an officer unless he is a paratrooper."

"Is it a rule?"

"We have no rules; let's say that it's a custom that has just been created. You had similar paratroop units in France. What became of them?"

"They no longer exist."

"Why not?"

"Perhaps it was thought that they could become dangerous. And in Israel?"

He shrugs his powerful shoulders. "In a way, we are all paratroopers here."

TRAINING

General Tsur, a former chief of staff and currently Moshe Dayan's Deputy Minister of Defense, tells me:

"War still remains for us a commando action enlarged to the dimensions of a classical war. Just as in a commando raid we must strike fast and hard. We are condemned to the

Blitzkrieg, that is, to attain by any and all means and very quickly the objective we have pinpointed for ourselves. From the brigade down to the platoon, all the units of the Israeli army act more or less according to the techniques and in the spirit of the commandos. The units can fight in isolation without fear, common in classical armies, of running out of provisions, ammunition, or water or of being deprived of their left or right flank, losing contact with other units, or no longer having artillery support. They improvise as the fighting goes on. Their strength depends entirely on their speed, their self-sufficiency, and their mobility. They never encumber themselves with unnecessary equipment. In a campaign there are no rear bases, no messes, no staff tents with huge maps marked up in red or blue pencil for the edification of newspapermen. There are neither hot meals nor settled arrangements. A general digs his own foxhole in the sand and shares his rations with his driver. We try above all to catch the enemy by surprise, as the commandos do. To surprise them, to strike, and to vanish. Our soldiers rush in where nobody expects them; they don't stop but advance constantly toward the objective to be attained. That objective is never the conquest of a stretch of ground but always the destruction of an enemy army. In the Tsahal, training is pushed so far that at any moment an officer can be replaced, without the slightest loss of momentum, by his next-in-command, then by the next, and so on down to the very lowest echelons.

"As in the commandos, the officers advance at the head of their men. They lead the same life that the men do; they have no special privileges. They have to be the best to be accepted as the real leaders of their platoons or companies. Our overall losses in officers are the highest in the world: 30 percent during the Six-Day War. But doesn't one find similar percentages in the commando units of all armies?"

General Sharon, on his part, tells me:

"In 1948, our soldiers could return from a mission without

having executed it: it was admitted that we were not yet an army. Today, I don't know of a single case in which a mission has not been completed, even if the losses were extremely heavy, even if the unit was completely destroyed. In 1948 the officers did not march at the head of their men. In 1956 it was already more common; in 1967, all of them did. These rules make up a part of the technique, the kind of fighting and the kind of esprit de corps of the commandos, and whoever says 'commando' is necessarily saying 'paratrooper.' It is the paratroopers, the paratrooper spirit, and paratroop training that have made the Israeli army what it is."

In 1968 the aim of paratroop training is to create not simply soldiers who are able to make jumps but fighters animated with an aggressive spirit, better trained and capable of taking part, with maximum effectiveness and minimum losses, in any kind of combat, day or night. They might just as well be called "shock units," "special forces," or "commando groups."

During the Six-Day War, the only thing resembling an airborne operation was the helicopter lifting of two companies of red berets behind enemy lines to destroy the artillery at Abu Aweigila. Jumps are no longer made in combat, except for certain special missions that have more to do with espionage than with warfare.

If one looks only at the actual jump training that the Israeli units receive, he sees nothing particularly new. I visited such training centers. Some of them had been set up by French instructors: There one saw such trappings as the wheel, the tower, and the aircraft fuselage mounted on blocks. To receive an Israeli paratrooper's certificate a man must make ten jumps, including three at night followed by marches of fifteen miles. At the end of each march a particularly difficult combat run awaits the man who wants to obtain his badge.

Combat training plays an infinitely greater role than jumping in the preparation of a paratrooper. If one were to seek the ancestors of the Israeli paratroopers, one would have to look among Orde Wingate's Midnight Brigades. Wingate was convinced, even back then, that a fighting man had to be accustomed to moving around and finding his way at night without difficulty, to fire rapidly and instinctively without having to aim, and to make use of any weapon, even an unfamiliar one that had just been captured from the enemy.

Men, especially when they are young, do not need much sleep, much less than is generally believed. They can be taught not to sleep, or to sleep very little. From the findings of certain doctors, Wingate was convinced that only the first hour of sleep counted. It was the deepest and most refreshing sleep; the rest was simply time lost. When he became a general and took command of the Chindits in Burma, he forced his commandos to break their sleeping patterns and to sleep only for an hour here and there, at any time of the day or night and in any position. Wingate also demanded total sobriety of his men. He believed that the fighting man should be lightly equipped and not loaded down with blankets, provisions, and enough camping paraphernalia to deform the backs of young Boy Scouts. They had to accustom themselves by degrees to eating very little, or better to find food on the spot. Instead of setting up tents they simply made themselves light shelters with vines and plaited bamboo or took shelter in caves.

Eventually the "night fighters," scattered in the jungle and very much fewer than their adversaries, were able—through surprise and concentration on sudden deadly hand-to-hand engagements—to create a sense of constant fear and insecurity in their enemy.

All this teaching remains, hardly changed at all, in the training of Israeli paratroopers. First, there is night combat. A considerable portion of the paratroopers' training takes place at night, not only jumps, but also marches and attacks on small forts and blockhouses. The paratrooper has to learn to know all of his country by night—and by night it is a different country. Israel is very small, but the paratroop units never stop crossing and recrossing the Galilee and the Negev, from the borders of Lebanon to those of Egypt. There is no ravine, village, kibbutz, or sand dune with which they do not become familiar in daylight or dark.

Next, there is the limitation of sleep. The paratrooper is trained to sleep no more than four hours a night. For six months he is led progressively to go without sleep and to sleep under any conditions, in a hole dug in the sand, under a tent cloth, or with nothing more than a rock for a pillow and a handkerchief over his head to avoid, as much as possible, being bitten by mosquitoes.

On one visit to Colonel Rafoul's paratroop brigade in the region of Jericho, I was struck by the brief time devoted to sleep in this unit. It was like being in ancient China, where the night was devoted to mah-jongg and the day to business. For military reasons—guarding the frontiers—but also for personal convenience and out of habit, everyone spends the night outdoors, on patrols, in ambush, talking, telephoning one another at impossible hours, drinking orange sodas—or remaking the world.

At 6:00 in the morning, after going to bed at 4:00, everybody is up for a breakfast of fried eggs, sliced cucumbers and tomatoes, and yogurt. Nobody shows a trace of fatigue.

General Uzi Harkiss, who commanded the troops that captured the Old City of Jerusalem, explains to me: "We have sought to create a type of soldier who thinks and acts particularly fast, living on his nerves and capable of going without sleep and food. Our discipline may seem rather slack because we never want a too-rigid discipline to work against the initiative of the individual. We have only accentuated certain aspects of that individual's temperament. The Jew has always been alert, high-strung, imaginative. Through intensive training we have bent him like a bow, to the point where he can sustain fatigue and lack of sleep beyond normal limits. Such tension cannot be sustained too long. I estimate that the elite Israeli soldier can last for two months of combat. We are consequently condemned to quick wars. The last one lasted six days."

Third, the Israeli paratroopers are veritable living encyclopedias of all the light weapons currently employed in the world. They are, in fact, taught to be familiar not only with Israeli arms but also with the British or American arms, with which the Jordanian and Iraqi armies are equipped, the Russian arms with which the Egyptians and the Syrians are equipped, the French arms used in Lebanon, and the Chinese arms given by Mao Tse-tung to the al-Fatah commandos. The instant that such a weapon is captured, the paratrooper must be able to turn it against the enemy and figure out how it works simply by touching it with his hands blindfolded. He may well find himself in this situation during a night fight.

The paratroop units that I visited had at their disposal a very wide choice of rifles, submachine guns, and machine guns, each man choosing for himself the weapon he considers the best. In general, the Soviet Kalachnikoff assault gun is most admired. It is sturdy, it fires very powerful ammunition, and it can be used as both a submachine gun and as an automatic rifle. Furthermore, it does not jam.

But I knew a tank officer at El Quneitra who collected weapons and who had a secret preference for a submachine gun, of Chinese manufacture, that looked like a string of hammered tin cans but had, so he told me, great advantages.

The paratrooper's target training is extremely intensive until he acquires that instinct that enables him to fire automatically without wasting time either raising his gun or aiming it.

The Israelis are not very rich. Their military budget of 11 percent of Gross National Income, one of the highest in the world (and this official figure is actually very much lower than the real one), seriously cripples the development of the country. Even so, they devote considerable sums to training their troops, especially in firearms; target shooting and hiking have become the most popular sports in Israel.

Fourth, the paratrooper is taught everything related to hand-to-hand combat: judo, close combat, knife throwing, how to crawl up to a sentinel without making a sound, and how to strangle him without his crying out. For reasons more psychological than military, great importance is given to hand-to-hand combat. And there, too, we find the influence of Wingate, who told the Jews: "The Arab is afraid of the dark: be soldiers of the night. The Arab is afraid of hand-to-hand combat and of the knife: fight with knives and hand-to-hand. He who frightens the other by playing on his weaknesses has won."

The Israeli paratroopers are taught always to seek out combat at close quarters: to hold their fire until the enemy is only a few yards away—or to wait for the enemy motionlessly and then to leap on him with a knife. An old tradition, more literary than real, attributed to the Arabs qualities that it generally denied the Jews: courage, a taste for blood and violence, and invincibility in close combat.

The myth of the irresistible Arab is one of the most cherished beliefs of the Christian peoples. It is fed by school-day memories of the Moslem conquests and the romantic epics of the Revolt in the Desert. We love to frighten ourselves by imagining a fanatical army of Arabs charging in the millions out of the desert to skewer the infidels to the cry of "Allah! Allah!" and I imagine that the idea of this fantom must have sprung up in the 11th century, during the first crusade (C. S. Jarvis, *Three Deserts,* London).

The Israeli paratroopers have turned this legend to their own advantage. Nowadays, the Arabs treat them with horror as butchers but at the same time reveal the ambivalence of their character, as General Yariv would say, by never ceasing in their propaganda, in print or on the radio, to exalt the butchery that they vow to inflict on all the Jews.

Terror has changed sides.

To find the roots of this brutal education of the Jewish fighter, it may be necessary to go farther back in time. The Jewish fighter certainly needed to prove, not only in the eyes of the world but above all in those of his Arab neighbors, his strength, his courage, and his manhood, even in their most primitive form: knife fighting.

Behind the young Israeli of 1968 are massed the shades of those millions of Jews who let themselves be pushed toward the crematory ovens without defending themselves. So today their sons, in order to forget this past, throw out their chests and brandish their daggers, as the Maccabees brandished their swords.

Fifth—and once again we can discern the teaching of Wingate—the Israeli soldier, particularly the paratrooper, must be capable at any moment of taking great initiative. His training prepares him to do so. Everything is explained to him in the most complete detail: The ideal is a curious, informed soldier, to whom one can always give orders on a higher level of sophistication than is possible with a private—or even a sergeant—in a Western army. In war this Israeli soldier—and the paratrooper is simply an upgraded infantryman—is kept abreast of all the details of the operation being carried out, of the movements of neighboring units, and so on.

A private can therefore replace an officer without grave dislocation. This tradition is both prudent and useful, for the officers are accustomed to going ahead of their men and thus to receiving the first enemy gun bursts.

Among the Israeli paratroopers there is only one absolute rule: "Even if everything goes wrong, even if the battalion is no longer commanded by anyone but a private, even if it no longer contains more than a handful of men, even if no one is going to come back alive, the mission will be executed."

Finally, the paratroopers also owe their special training for survival in the desert, or on enemy territory, to Wingate. In Israel there is a survival school like the one in Panama for the American special forces. All the paratroopers—and pilots,

before they fly, have been paratroopers for a year and a half
—learn to "pick over" the desert, that is, to find where nothing appears to grow roots that give a kind of milk and berries
that appease hunger. They know how to make a smokeless
fire, how to make a canteen of water last indefinitely, how
to cool it by evaporation, how to catch certain edible snakes,
how to hide by day and move by night, how to weave themselves fiber blankets.

In the course of certain exercises they are dropped in the
middle of the night far from any village in the Negev, for
example, alone and equipped with only a canteen of water
and a compass. They must find their way back to their bases,
sometimes after walking several days.

COLONEL RAFUL SPEAKS

One of the most respected paratroopers in Israel is Colonel
Raful, aged thirty-eight. Nobody knows how many times he
has been wounded; he has more scars than an old alley cat.
He is a short, aggressive man who likes challenge; he is
known for his toughness in combat, his cynical tongue, and
his courage. His men would follow him to hell, because, one
of them said, "it's hard to picture Raful in heaven."

*I am lunching with the Colonel at his headquarters near
Jericho. He is surrounded by a group of his officers, who
imitate his posture and have the same gestures, the same
lean faces, the same glittering wolf's eyes.*

*"The training of our paratroopers," Raful tells me, "has a
double aim. First, to make it possible for them to fight,
through their training, tricks and stratagems, you know.
That's the easiest part. And also to incite in them a genuine
desire to fight. That's a lot harder.*

*"We don't have to instill love of their country in our para-
troopers. They have it in their blood. But we have to develop
in them at the same time the cult of honor and esprit de*

corps. Esprit de corps, with us, is based on the feeling of solidarity that exists among all the men of the same unit, no matter what their ranks and duties are.

"The officer commands, not by giving orders but by his personal example. This is why he must always be the first to set an example, even that of dying.

"We insist that all officers must pass through all the levels of the paratrooper hierarchy, that they lead exactly the same life as the privates, that they sleep with them, eat with them, talk things over with them. In order that this feeling of solidarity may remain strong, we avoid changes and transfers within companies as much as possible.

"For a year and a half, recruits will remain in the same company, taking their entire training together, getting to know one another very well, becoming bound to one another. Then the company is dissolved; some men go to officers' or warrant officers' schools, others become instructors, and the least promising are assigned to another unit.

"The first part of a paratrooper's training lasts six months— three months of classwork, let's say of the rudiments, and three months of jump training, with a certificate at the end. Then the training continues: It will, in fact, never cease. We must make our men know the whole of Israel, make them cover it all on foot. The aim of this training is to see to it that when it is finished anyone can replace anyone else, in any job."

All the paratroopers are, of course, volunteers. They often come from kibbutzim or moshavim. They are consequently sturdy fellows, animated by a strong patriotism. Even so the training is so hard that more than a quarter of them flunk out.

I ask the colonel to give me a picture of the Israeli para- trooper.

"He is a soldier," he replies, "whose intensive training has endowed him with very highly developed physical capabil- ities, who knows thoroughly how to use the terrain and the potentials of the weapons that he will have to use, whether *his own or the enemy's, who has the will to fight and fights. And it is for all these reasons—and some others—that the Israeli paratrooper is the best in the world."*

"Do you think he is?"

"One must say it to believe it and believe it to become it."

PARATROOPERS IN ACTION

The paratroop units are generally organized in brigades commanded by a colonel. In general, the brigade plays the role of an administrative unit. Its battalions subdivide into various units or groups according to the needs of the moment and the necessities of combat.

The reconnaissance formation of Sharon's group in the Sinai thus included a company of tanks, a company of jeeps carrying paratroopers, a unit of engineers, and a battalion of paratroopers.

It can also happen that a brigade of paratroopers may function as an autonomous group, as was the case during the Sinai campaign of 1956. Moshe Dayan gave us the composition of such a group: three battalions of paratroopers, two companies of the Nahal (who are also paratroopers), a squadron of AMX tanks, a battery of field artillery, and a battery of heavy mortars. When its complement is up to full strength, that paratroop battalion of four companies numbers about 600 men, 150 to each company.

The paratroopers have been trained to such a high degree of mobility that in 1967 one brigade, after having fought the entire Sinai campaign, returned under its own power from the banks of the Suez Canal to attack the Syrian positions on the Golan Heights.

The most impartial judgment of the Israeli paratroopers can come only from an enemy. Let us, then, hear from an Egyptian colonel who was taken prisoner in the battle of Abu Aweigila:

"We had concentrated all our forces, including tanks and

big guns facing forward, to the west. We were stupefied when your soldiers erupted into the trenches on our flanks, at the very moment when your tanks were charging us from in front. The enemy is so light of foot that in the twinkling of an eye he was upon me" (Ben Elissar and Schiff, *La guerre*).

We are going to see these paratroopers at work in Jerusalem—in a struggle in which they can hardly be supported by planes, artillery, and tanks.

By attacking first on June 5, 1967, the Jews immediately set a number of governments against them: those of Charles de Gaulle, who had expressly asked them to avoid armed conflict and who felt that he had been "let down"; of Lyndon B. Johnson, who made no concrete proposal to reopen the Strait of Tiran but asked all parties to wait for the U.N. to come up with something resembling a settlement; of the British, traditional protectors of the Arabs, their old lovers who had been "stolen away" by the Russians but for whom they still had tender feelings; the Russians and all the countries of East Europe except for the Rumanians, who had already established their autonomy from Moscow, and the Czechs, who were beginning to establish theirs.

In taking the additional risk of destroying or damaging the holy places, the Jews did not intend to provoke the armed reactions of all the Christian countries, including those like the U.S.S.R. that might find themselves still Christian for the occasion.

The Israeli paratroopers of Colonel Mordechai Gur, nicknamed Motta, were this time face to face with a solid and well-commanded force that had not been stupefied by political propaganda or divided by factional feuds, plots, and military coups d'état: the Arab Legion of King Hussein of Jordan.

The Israelis naturally expected a response from King Hussein in case of war, but they did not anticipate that he would actually intervene alongside Nasser, in spite of all the treaties signed and promises made. Moshe Dayan, and in this he is very much the student of Ben-Gurion, has always scorned the Arabs, which he calls "taking them at their own estimate." Before he became Minister of Defense he advised General Uzi Narkiss, commander of Israel's central zone: "In case of a heavy strike, don't falter. It's unlikely that the Jordanians will be seriously aroused. Let them make their fighting gesture of honor. Don't ask for reinforcements, and send as many of your lads as possible into the Sinai. That's where all the action will be" (Cuau, *Israël attaque*).

A few days later, when he had assumed his ministerial functions, he repeated to Narkiss: "Don't bother the general staff with requests for reinforcements. Grind your teeth, and say nothing."

Jordanian intervention was all the more surprising because it would take place at a time when all the Egyptian aircraft had already been destroyed. The first shots were fired by the Arab Legion on Monday about 10:30 A.M., when Nasser's airfields were already in flames. The Israeli Foreign Minister instantly sent King Hussein a message through General Odd Bull, head of the U.N. observers, asking him not to intervene in the conflict. In return, Israel gave assurances that it would not act against him either in Jordan or in Jerusalem. But, if he were to ignore this warning, "Israel will react with extreme violence, and King Hussein will have to take the consequences."

For it took all Hussein's stubbornness, as well as all his loyalty toward his pathetic Egyptian ally and all his ignorance of the latest developments in the air war, to enable the Jews to capture the Old City of Jerusalem and the holy places—to realize the dread of 2,000 years and officially end the Diaspora. "*This* year in Jerusalem," people could now say in their prayers.

The opening gunshots were, however, followed by a thorough bombardment from big guns and mortars. General Narkiss—he told me so himself—was no longer happy. He understood that the Jordanians were not going to limit themselves to an honorific fighting gesture, that they were going too far. He telephoned his friend Teddy Kollek, Mayor of the Israeli sector of Jerusalem, "Those Jordanian imbeciles are absolutely bent on making you the mayor of reunified Jerusalem."

The Jordanians really did go too far when they occupied Government House, which stood between the two lines and had become U.N. headquarters; when they announced, as if it had already been accomplished—though it never was to be accomplished at all—the taking of Mount Scopus, which overlooks all Jerusalem; and when they bombarded several kibbutzim in Galilee.

The general staff then agreed in principle to action against Jordan and an attack on the Old City of Jerusalem. Narkiss had very few troops at his disposal: the Jerusalem brigade of Colonel Amitai (2,500 men, of whom many were students) and the armored brigade of Colonel Ben Ari, made up of reservists (2,500 men) and equipped with Shermans, Pattons, a few Centurions and two or three Fouga-Magisters converted into ground-support planes. At the last moment Narkiss was given a reduced brigade of paratroopers—1,500 men, commanded by Colonel Gur.

On the afternoon before the attack on the Old Town Motta's paratroopers lay flat in the grass next to the runway of an airport near Tel Aviv waiting for Nord-Atlases to pick them up and drop them over the Sinai. The colonel and his officers were standing guard around the telephone. Would it ring or not? Would they jump or not? Since 1956, when only one small unit commanded by Sharon had parachuted in to close the Mitla Pass, no Israeli had made an operational jump. Everyone envied the few select men who were entitled to wear their insignia on a red background.

The waiting grew aggravating. At 2:00 P.M. the order came to detach a battalion from the brigade to Jerusalem, and instead of the Nord-Atlases, old buses turned up.

COLONEL GUR NARRATES

"The men, dismayed, immediately realized that with one less battalion the chances of a parachute operation were diminished. I went at once to General Narkiss and learned that it was no longer one battalion but two that had to be ordered to Jerusalem without delay. And even before I could get back to the airfield other orders had already preceded me. The whole brigade was to move out toward the capital, with one of the most difficult missions possible: to break through enemy defenses on fortified terrain, with a primary objective of effecting a rendezvous with the Israeli unit on Mount Scopus—about six miles from the city—and a secondary aim of setting ourselves up in such a way as to be able to launch an assault on the Old City of Jerusalem" (Ben Elissar and Schiff, *La guerre israëlo-arabe*).

When the paratroopers learned of their new mission, to take the Holy City, they quickly forgot their disappointment. Instead of a red patch under a pair of silver wings, instead of a dangerous jump into the sands of the desert, they were being offered the noblest fight a Jewish soldier could make: to conquer the city of David and Solomon with the Wailing Wall, the golden city enclosed by Suleiman the Magnificent. The brigade marched off singing, as if for a celebration or a procession.

Motta left with his commanders to reconnoiter the ground. He was afraid that his paras might get lost in the meandering streets of the city, and he detailed a certain number of soldiers of the Jerusalem brigade to act as guides. Mortar shells did not stop raining down. There were wounded and killed. Motta set up headquarters in a private house of the corner of Tsafania Street. The brigade entered Jerusalem at about 5:00 P.M. from the west, in the Beth Hakerem quarter, and began to deploy. The platoon leaders and company com-

manders went up close to the line of demarcation and recon-
noitered their bases of departure for the attack.

As Motta described the plan, "Night falls swiftly in our
part of the world, and it was by the light of torches that the
officers, leaning over maps, gave out brief and precise instructions. Two battalions were to launch an attack on the
enemy: One was to head for the sector of the police school
and Munitions Hill; the other was to advance toward the
Sheikh Jarrah quarter. Since no one could say what the cost
of the battle would be, I set up a system of rapid evacuation
of the wounded."

The hour for the attack was set for 7:00 the following
morning—but General Narkiss decided otherwise. It began
at 2:00 in the morning. When I asked him why he had gone
so far as to ignore the orders of the general staff, he answered
as if he had acted quite normally:

"It has always been said that our soldiers fight better at
night than by day. Then why not take advantage of the
night? At the end of the day I called together the chiefs of
battalions, and it was they who said to me: 'Uzi, now is the
time to move, before the other side receives reinforcements.
We feel it and all our men feel it: The Jordanians are letting
go a little. By tomorrow morning they'll be all pulled together
again. We mustn't let the opportunity go by.'"

According to Motta, "At 2:20 A.M. the Israeli tanks began
to move forward under a heavy artillery barrage; at the same
moment the paratroopers launched their attack on the first
networks of barbed wire that divided the city in two.

"Dead and wounded men dropped pell-mell. The
wounded, who were evacuated fastened to stretchers, were
furious at being taken out of the fight 'like that, for nothing,'
without even a chance to fire their Uzis or throw some grenades. The struggle was extraordinarily bitter, and the battle
surpassed in fury anything that can be imagined. It must not
be forgotten that the men had to confront, on one side, a
broken terrain in which the enemy was solidly entrenched

and, on the other, a built-up zone where every house, every rooftop, every cellar might be a pocket of resistance. Often the men had to cut through five successive barbed-wire barriers *and* clear a path through the minefields that separated them."

During the night, Hussein's Bedouin Legionnaires met the paratroopers in a succession of furious hand-to-hand struggles. The paratroopers blew up bunkers with explosive charges and were themselves blown up by mines, for there was not a single "frying pan" in Jerusalem with which to clear away mines. They had all been sent into the Sinai. It was during the attack on Munitions Hill, the real barrier to Jerusalem, that the fighting was the hardest and the losses most severe.

"Such-and-such a commander attained his objective with just four soldiers left from his company, and such-and-such another with only seven out of his platoon, without ever at any moment sending me any other message than 'Evacuate the wounded!' "

Nir, the assistant to a commander of one company, tells of how, while standing on the edge of a trench, he saw one of his men who had been wounded in the hip continuing to fire a machine gun: "Blood flowed freely, and the wound was deep. I stuck my finger in to stop the flood. My man was quite unaware of anything, and I almost had to force him to be evacuated by the only medic I had left."

The police school, held by 200 Jordanian Legionnaires, resisted several furious assaults by the paratroopers. It was not until 4:00 A.M. that the former surrendered, in the light of floodlights set up on the top of an apartment building. One hundred six Jordanians were dead, and all the rest were wounded. The Israeli brigade lost a quarter of its officers that night.

All day Tuesday the paratroopers cleaned out the Jordanian quarters that they had just taken, but from atop the ramparts of the Old City and the Mount of Olives the Arab

Legion continued artillery bombardment of the Israeli position. The Mount of Olives was taken by two squadrons of Israeli tanks, as was Augusta Victoria Hill, but a counter-attack by Jordanian tanks dislodged them.

On Wednesday morning General Narkiss called Motta on the telephone: "Faster! The faster the operations are completed, the better it will be for Israel."

And, indeed, the Security Council was meeting in New York, and doing its utmost to obtain a cease-fire.

After an aerial bombardment the two hills were retaken. The Old City was surrounded. The order for the assault was given after a violent artillery barrage on the Moslem quarters between the Damascus Gate and St. Stephen's Gate; it was very brief, lasting scarcely ten minutes.

It was 10:12 A.M.

"Already, at the end of the road," Motta continued, "St. Stephen's Gate was in sight. One side of it was open. A burning vehicle barred the entrance. I said to my driver: 'Charge! Let's go, Ben Zur!'

"It was necessary to charge, it was necessary to take risks, it was necessary to get there. Ben Zur stepped on the gas, passed the burning vehicle, smashed into the door, which shattered, and crushed the stones that blocked the way. A few hundred yards still separated us from Mount Moriah and the esplanade of the former Temple. We rushed down the street, passing on our left the fortress of Antonia, which marks the beginning of the Via Dolorosa (Street of Sorrows). There we turned sharp left, to find a gate that gave access at last to the holy of holies. An abandoned motorcycle blocked the entrance.

"Was it booby-trapped or wasn't it?

"Ben Zur accelerated and mashed the motorcycle; the door opened."

A paratrooper named Zamouche was the first to arrive before the Wailing Wall; on its top he planted a flag that he had brought from his kibbutz. One of his buddies, who was carrying a bottle of wine in his haversack, broke it at the neck and passed it around among his fellows, who repeated one after the other as they drank: "To life! *This* year in Jerusalem!"

Jordanian soldiers who had taken cover in houses or behind low terrace walls were still firing when bearded Rabbi Shlomo Goren, out of breath and weeping, rushed to the Wall and kissed it. Then he blew the ram's horn and intoned the prayers, which were taken up by all those paratroopers, very few of whom were practicing Jews: "Blessed be Thou, Eternal God, Who hast given us life that we might know such a moment."

The paratroopers of Israel had just written, in two days of fighting, the most glorious page of the war and of the history of the Jewish people.

THE NAHAL

The Nahal, possessing dual military-civilian status, composed of 60 percent young men and 40 percent young women, a corps of military pioneers charged with clearing new lands, as well as with night combat and guarding the frontiers, is unique in the world. These pioneers are saturated in the thinking of the paratroopers, for all the boys put in a long hitch in the airborne troops—they must have jumping certificates—and practically all their military instructors come from the paratroops.

The Nahal is the holy of holies of the army and the kibbutzim at once, a sort of laboratory for constructing a new kind of human being. It is, alas, only a laboratory, for, in spite of all that Ben-Gurion did to encourage them, the members of the Nahal are still very few in number.

They depend on the army for their training, their supplies, their arms, and their discipline. The general staff decides on the particular spots where they will establish new outposts, and in such decisions strategic considerations always take precedence over all others.

But each new military colony will be "adopted" by a kibbutz in its general vicinity, which will lend it assistance, send it advisers, give it seeds, share farm machinery. The Nahal boys and girls are often inexperienced in agriculture: They generally come from the cities. The Nahal colony will be, first of all, a guard post and a strong point in a zone of insecurity, or in occupied territory; only when relative security has been established and after intensive agricultural exploitation of a collective character for two or three years, will it in turn be converted into a kibbutz. Its insignia: a parachute and a sickle.

Paul Ginievski gives reasons for the creation of the Nahal in 1949.

The State of Israel is of a unique smallness and shape. Its vital centers are a few minutes' flight from Arab territories; if a break occurs on the front, tanks can, in a few hours, attack Tel Aviv, coming from Nablus or from El 'Arish. The parliament in Jerusalem is within range of automatic rifles on the Jordanian battlements of the Old City. Under these conditions, the frontiers being in addition immeasurably lengthened by their winding course constantly doubling back on themselves, only a "hedgehog" defense—unbroken crossfire by groups stationed over the entire terrain—can make for an effective resistance against an enemy who has scored a breakthrough. This consideration has, since 1947, continued to influence the plan for developing the country, and the hundreds of new villages of Galilee, the corridor, and the Negev bear witness to it. The importance of strategic colonization to the safety of Israel explains the Nahal. (Paul Ginievski, *Le Bouclier de David*, Paris: Berger-Levrault)

Israel's strategic situation is no longer the same; it has enlarged its frontiers. And it is in these newly occupied territories (which the Israelis do not seem to be in any hurry to give back, for they are setting up military colonies in them) that the two Nahal colonies I visited are located.

One of them, Nahal Yam, is in the Sinai, by the sea between El 'Arish and El Qantara. The other, Nahal Golan, is, as its name indicates, on Syrian territory, on the Golan Heights.

Here is how a Nahal colony is born. A group of boys and girls who have known one another from early childhood— have been together in school, which is always coeducational, have enrolled in the same youth movement (every political party has one), and have undergone their Gadna military training together—decide to become pioneers, kibbutz-dwellers. They then form a nucleus, a "cell."

These cells are almost always formed in the big cities. It is the "call of the West," the lure of adventure for young city-dwellers who dream of doing more, of going farther than others in the building of Israel. When they reach the age of eighteen, they ask to take their military service together.

First they are sent off to take courses—the boys for four months and the girls for two. Then the girls go home and wait until their comrades have finished their training, which is more complete.

They are then reunited and sent to an established kibbutz, where they learn communal living in relative comfort for six months; next they go to a new kibbutz, where the facilities are still rudimentary and life difficult.

Then, once again, the "cell" separates. The young men go off for six months in a paratroop unit, where their training is particularly "careful"—that is, exceptionally rough.

I was present at the graduation ceremony of some Nahal paratroopers. I talked with their officers, who were hard-boiled old professionals. They boasted to me of the quality and the endurance of these boys—and of their humor. A person enters a Nahal colony as he would enter a kibbutz; that is, as one enters a religious order. Individual freedom, money, and the ambition that must be renounced are compensated for, in general, by a certain insouciance and *joie de vivre*.

The young people of the Nahal gave me an example of this

humor through some skits that they put on for their instructors, in which they made fun of them—not without crude-
ness.

Meanwhile the girls take a certain number of courses in
which they learn everything that a pioneer woman needs to
know—cooking no less than dietetics, sewing as well as the
repair of jeep or truck motors and how to drive a tractor.

All together again, the "cell" is assigned to a spot where it
is to establish itself; then the great adventure begins under
the tents. Or it may be sent to replace another "cell" that is
migrating elsewhere. After a year the members of the "cell"
establish themselves as a kibbutz. Some of them find that the
life doesn't suit them and go home.

In the Nahal boys and girls live in separate barracks. They
are constantly together in the dining hall, working in the
fields, in the common room. Their life is exhausting, which
greatly reduces sexual problems. In any case, in the Nahal
there are no couples and no children. (The State of Israel
has, from its beginnings, permitted all forms of contraception,
to the detriment, of course, of population growth, which is
one of the burning issues in the country.)

Nahal Yam has been established in the Sinai in the midst
of the desert near a railway line along the seacoast; the sands
are still strewn with the blackened wrecks of ammunition
convoys blown up by Israeli aircraft. About twenty barracks
are surrounded by networks of barbed wire and lit at night
by floodlights. It is very hot in the daytime and cool at night,
as in the Sahara. But here air conditioning is unknown.

Before us is the lake of Sabkha, which is linked to the
Mediterranean by way of two channels. This lake, which is
hardly more than six feet deep, is very rich in fish. The new
Nahal colony will devote itself to fishing, which once occupied 500 to 600 people here. There is no choice! Fish are the
sole resource of the area.

The boats have arrived, and the nets too, along with some
fishermen from Lake Tiberias and the Elath region, who are

to serve as advisers. But the boats have too deep a draft and the engines get stuck on the bottom; it is also necessary to rediscover the fishing places that the Bedouin keep secret.

The girls take care of all the domestic work and provisions, raising a few livestock, some chickens, and several tomato patches. During the Sinai campaign two members of a kibbutz captured a strange apparatus mounted on wheels and the size of a large truck. Manufactured partly in East Germany and partly in Italy, it had been given to the Egyptians by the Russians to desalinate sea water. Its captors gave it to Nahal Yam. The apparatus, which roars all night long, is used only to water the precious tomatoes, which are protected against the encroachments of the sand by high reed windbreakers. It cannot supply drinking water and consumes almost as much gasoline as it produces water. I dare not guess the price of a pound of those tomatoes.

Nahal Yam is commanded by a lieutenant of the regular army. He explains to me that the region is relatively calm but that al-Fatah men, coming from the direction of the sea, planted mines on the road two days ago: Three people were killed and six wounded.

While waiting for fishing to begin in earnest, the young men guard the channels, keep watch over the coast, go on patrols, and control the few tribes of Bedouin who live in the dunes on the desert side. Israelis are trying to persuade the latter to accept identity cards by linking them with fishing permits.

The boys are outdoors part of the night; the girls stand guard during the first two hours, from 8:00 P.M. to 10:00 P.M. Nahal Yam is always on the alert. I am, furthermore, awakened in the middle of the night by an exercise. The next day, while driving toward El Qantara, a few miles from Nahal Yam, I see a command car that has exploded on the road—and realize that in the Sinai a practice alert can very easily become a real action.

Nahal Yam must be able to hold out with its own resources, until morning if it is attacked. Its defenses: a few holes in the sand and a few mortar emplacements and automatic weapons.

The other Nahal colony is in the north, on the Syrian Golan Heights, astride the new boundaries of Syria, Jordan, and Israel. All the members of this colony come from the city. Their patrons are the big kibbutzim of the Jordan valley. The location is even more "unhealthy" than the Sinai. In front of each barracks stands a shelter with plank walls cemented with mud. Three months ago Nahal Golan was attacked with bazookas by Palestinian commandos, and a girl lost a leg. A plastic bomb exploded in a watercloset. The day before my arrival a tractor was blown up by a mine.

Night has scarcely fallen when the boom of artillery is heard, and rocket flares light up the horizon. On the terrace of an Arab house, converted into a watch tower and equipped with a spotlight and a heavy machine gun, I chat with the two lieutenants in command of the post.

One of them comes from a kibbutz in the Negev and intends to remain here when the colony becomes a kibbutz in turn. The other, who wears an "Indian army" moustache, has no other plan than to carve out a career in the army.

The kibbutz dweller speaks with love of the very rich land that surrounds the post (it is, nevertheless, Syrian territory).

Counting on his fingers like a peasant, he explains: "We already cultivate 286 acres of sorghum, 66 acres of watermelons, 66 acres of sunflowers, and 4.5 acres of tomatoes. We are expecting 250 head of sheep and 400 chickens. Everything grows here. The earth has only been scratched—and the Syrians declared it a military zone and forbade the peasants to come here."

I find it hard to imagine this soldier-peasant torn from this land, which he already loves with that zeal for possession of the soil that is the property of all kibbutz dwellers.

Did not all the tractors of the valley kibbutzim arrive in long files the minute the fighting on the Golan Height was over? Advancing, they stretched in a single line for miles across the plateau still strewn with the blackened wreckage of weapons and with corpses. They had taken possession of it in their own way by giving it new life.

The military man, worried about "all that racket" on the frontier, only a mile or two away, telephones brigade headquarters. For the moment, there is nothing in particular to report. The flares have been fired by the Syrians; they seem to have huge stocks of them, as they waste so many. The big guns are Jordanian, and they too do not lack ammunition. The lieutenant offers me a cigarette and props himself up on a parapet of sandbags. I ask him how the tractor was blown up.

"Simple negligence," he tells me. "Every morning we open up the roads and clear the fields of mines. Yesterday the mine-cleaning team was late. The tractor guy and his pal were in a hurry to go attend to their plants. They left at 5:00 in the morning. There was a mine in the field, more than a pound of plastic. It had been placed there during the night. They are all around us, you know, and they come and go pretty much as they like between patrols. The tractor was wrecked. But the men were all right. They got off with being tossed into the watermelons."

"How much time do your men sleep?"

"With all these patrols, watches, perpetual alerts, barely four hours."

"And the girls?"

"They have to make coffee and meals for the men coming back from patrol duty, and they work in the fields. Like the men, hardly any more."

The watch-tower spotlight lingers over the barbed-wire defenses of Nahal Golan. Flares still light up the sky; the big guns still grumble. I want to ask the two lieutenants how long this war will last. It's useless. The answer has already been given to me by other lieutenants, privates, colonels, and generals: "As long as Israel lasts. Forever."

Women and Children

What a strange army is this army of Israel, in which no outward sign, except some shoulder patches, distinguishes the officer from the soldier. Dressed in the same uniform and almost always bareheaded, they address each other familiarly. (The formal address similar to the French *vous* does not exist in Hebrew. The academy charged with modernizing the language wanted to introduce it, but encountered such strong opposition among the population that it had to renounce the attempt.) They hitchhike together. Incidentally, it seems that one of the main activities of the Tsahal, night and day, in wartime as in peacetime, is thumbing rides from passing cars on all the roads of Israel.

In Israel, the officers come from all walks of life. Far from constituting a closed caste, they are an integral part of the people. For the most part reservists, they never lose contact with the masses, with the man in the street.

The Arab officers, by contrast, consider themselves members of a privileged class. Coming, as a rule, from a comfortable background, middle-class or rich, they are destined for military careers in the diplomatic service. The majority of the Egyptian generals taken prisoner in the Sinai did not even know the names of their company commanders (Ben Elissar and Schiff, *La guerre israëlo-arabe*).

The Tsahal is an equilitarian army, the army of a classless country, and is strongly marked by the spirit of the kibbutzim, in which every leader is elected to every post by the general assembly of all the members. Things are almost exactly the same for the young officer. After four weeks all the recruits are given a questionnaire in which they are asked: "Among the comrades around you, which ones would you like to have as officers? As noncommissioned officers?" This nominating system was customary in the Palmach units, and the tradition has been preserved.

WOMEN SOLDIERS

But what particularly gives the Israeli army its orginality is the presence of women in all its units. They were with the tanks at El Quneitra, with the paratroopers in the Sinai, on the Jordan with the Golani Brigade. They can, furthermore, never be fewer than fifteen in number and are always administered by their own officers, women like themselves.

In Israel, all girls are mobilized between the ages of eighteen and twenty for twenty months' service. Postponements can be granted until the age of twenty-six. Arab propaganda comments ironically, with a certain envy and very bad taste, on this army "which is nothing but a vast bordello, in which every soldier finds always at his side the means of gratifying his lust." Mobilization of women is just as revolting to the Orthodox Jews, who see it as evidence of the corruption of the new state, and to some Oriental Jews who are still filled with the notion of the inferiority of women. The Yemenite Jews, for example, still believe that a woman is an inferior being who must never be allowed to go without a master. After her father, it is her brother, her uncle, or her husband; even as a widow, she falls back under the yoke of the family. By contrast, modern Israelis, sabras or not, find it completely normal that women should be mobilized. For equal rights, equal duties; for equal work, equal pay—so, roughly, says the constitution, or at least what passes for one. As the man undergoes military service, the woman must therefore also submit to the same obligation.

One of the colonels responsible for army training told me: "The kind of relations that exist in the Tsahal between girls and boys, friendly relations that are much more naïve and straightforward than anyone would believe, give the young girl—especially if she comes from an Oriental community—a feeling of equality and self-confidence that she is very far from having when she begins her training. She has been accustomed to consider herself inferior to men. The soldier who encounters her every day, wearing the same uniform and performing just about the same tasks, becomes used to thinking of her as a comrade and an equal. The girl soldier constantly reminds him of his reasons for fighting. If I were asked, 'From where does the Tsahal derive its strength?' I would reply, 'From the presence of women in the army'."

Paul Ginievski has written:

The problems of promiscuity among the boys and girls, first of all, does not arise at all in this country, where children, adolescents, and young adults are accustomed to coeducation at all ages. It follows that the relations between girls and boys in the Israeli army are exactly as good (or as bad), as pure (or as impure) as outside the army, with this difference: that in the army they are infinitely busier, infinitely more tired, infinitely less free than outside it, and that in consequence they "behave better."

In 1943, thirty-one Jews parachuted into Poland, Rumania, and Hungary to organize anti-Nazi resistance movements. Among them were women like Hannah Szenej, who was captured, tortured, and executed by the Germans. She was twenty-three years old. She declared to her tribunal: "I asked to be parachuted into Hungary to take arms in my hand against the German Nazis. Palestine has taught me to be free and proud of my Jewish origin. I have only done my duty."

During the war of independence in 1948, a few women fought in the ranks of the Haganah. Some were killed in combat. Others, like those twenty young women of Kefar Etzion, blew themselves up with their last remaining grenades rather than fall into the hands of the Arab Legion. Still others were active in the underground or terrorist movements—transporting weapons, making grenades in cellars, collecting intelligence, carrying bombs. Several hundred were killed.

As the Haganah was transformed into a regular army, the women moved back from the first line to the second. During the Sinai campaign in 1956, the only women soldiers who were killed died in automobile accidents. In 1967 the feminine army suffered only one loss during the Six-Day War: a young girl killed in a bombardment.

Although women no longer serve in the first-line fighting units, they nevertheless undergo combat training. After entering the service they spend five weeks in a camp near Tel Aviv, on the dunes along the seacoast. They live in barracks but also sleep in tents next to the firing range and the exercise ground. They have already been taught to march and how to use weapons. Haven't they already put in three years of military training in the Gadna? But now they receive more thorough training.

I have seen them firing submachine guns, these recruits who, they told me, had just arrived in camp. They carried and handled their weapons like old soldiers. They were already capable of marching twenty-five miles at a stretch. They were being taught to find their bearings in the wilderness, to dig trenches, to camouflage themselves, to throw hand grenades, to survive in the desert, to defend themselves in close combat. Their military training was roughly on a par with that of a male recruit of the French army in 1968.

They are also given some idea of administration. The general organization of the army is explained to them so that they can find their way about in it. And they are trained in first aid, in order to give preliminary care to the wounded.

When this first stage is over, they are transferred to various auxiliary services, where they receive specialized training as secretaries, telephone operators, bookkeepers, military policewomen, nurses, parachute packers, radar operators, radio transmitters, drivers, mechanics or supply officers. Others are sent to the frontier villages as instructors or to youth centers as training advisers. On the other hand, they are never assigned to the kitchens except in the military colonies of the Nahal. Cooking in Israel, in the army anyway, is considered too arduous a task for a woman.

Of the 60,000 soldiers who make up the active army, only a third are women. In the younger generation the percentage of boys is higher than that of girls, but if the recruiting regulations were strictly applied, the girls would make up at least 45 percent of the army. Clearly, exemptions from military service are numerous.

Exemptions are granted upon request to all girls from Orthodox religious families who regard it as a sacrilege to put these "fragile, inconstant, and irresponsible" beings among men; all married women; all those whose families are in difficult circumstances; and all those whose health or physical resistance is below par or who, after examination, seem likely to have a hard time coping with military life. This weeding-out process is, in fact, pretty ruthless.

Six months before the girls are to don uniforms, army social workers study them in relation to their respective family and social milieus. They have already been labeled, observed, tested in every possible way all during their Gadna training. The girls do everything they possibly can to be admitted into the army, and some rejections precipitate floods of tears and even nervous breakdowns. For it is hard to imagine a young Israeli, the hard-headed sabra with his frank and often crude manners, encumbering himself with a girl who has been judged not fit for military service.

Military service for women corresponds to very specific needs of the country. In wartime, women must be able to replace men wherever the latter's presence is not absolutely necessary. In view of Israel's 2.2 million inhabitants and its low percentage of young people (sabras have few children), the Israeli army must make use of all available human resources at its disposal, in order to line up the greatest possible number of fighters against the surrounding Arab countries.

For women, military service plays an important educational role as well. During periods of heavy immigration, the army was able to train quite a few young women in skills that they had never acquired. Among other things, they were taught Hebrew. Through contact with young women who had been born in Palestine, immigrant girls were freed of a great many taboos and were tempered in the great melting pot of the army: They became Israelis. It was enough to teach them that they finally had a country and therefore duties to it. This double ideal of patriotism and public service had previously been totally foreign to them. They were also taught courage. In a country of pioneers, a country constantly threatened, there is no place for fretful mothers who tremble every time their sons cross the street. It is because of its women, above all, that Israel can be compared to Sparta.

Once her military service is over, a young woman goes into the reserves until she is thirty-four. She does active duty for ten days each year, sometimes longer, even if she is married —but only if she has no children.

Within the Israeli army the women constitute a separate corps, with their own officers, their own administration, and their own discipline. Even when they are detached for service with distant units, where they are surrounded by men, they still take orders only from women officers, who alone can take disciplinary action against them.

COLONEL LEVY SPEAKS

The commander in chief of all the women soldiers of Israel is Colonel Stella Levy, who created the corps. She has a strong, lean face under close-cropped gray hair, but her myopic eyes are almost tender. Her body is thin and vigorous under her light-colored dress uniform.

Stella Levy speaks perfect French, as well as English, German, and Arabic. Alert and intelligent—very intelligent—she has a feeling for publicity and an easy manner that have made her a frequent public speaker. In times of peace, she travels all over the world to persuade international public opinion of the justice of her country's political position. As commander in chief of all the women soldiers of Israel she is manna from heaven to journalists, and she takes advantage of this situation in order to help her country.

I meet her in the camp where young girls who have just been called to the colors take their five-week basic training. She has just come back from a tour of the United States, "which was a success." She spreads out before me a pile of newspaper clippings and photographs. "Not too great, these photographs," she says, with some satisfaction, nevertheless. "Above all, please don't read my biography; it's completely fictitious."

Here, then, is just about all that is known of Stella Levy, except for her age, which is never mentioned anywhere and which, with a coquetry that is very feminine and not at all military, she neglects to tell me. She was born in Israel, of parents who themselves had been born there: She is a sabra and the daughter of sabras. She is married to an engineer who is a sabra himself, but they have no children.

In 1942 she enlisted in the British army. "I took my classes in this same camp," she tells me. "It hasn't changed much in twenty-five years. There are still the same wooden barracks and the same grillwork which theoretically—very theoretically—separates the men's and women's quarters."

She points to some disheveled young faces, which are visible through the windows. They are topped by kibbutz hats in the shape of upside-down bells—the "clown's cap," as it is called. The girls are pushing and shoving like schoolgirls.

"They've only been here six days, and, as you see, they're completely at ease. When they arrived they were as stiff as pokers and stared at their feet instead of looking me in the eye. Their transformation is quite mysterious. And every time it's the same. Perhaps they feel liberated at last from the yoke of family, custom, a sometimes suffocating social milieu. The first thing they learn here is freedom.

"In my day the barracks were the same, though newer, but the British WACs hardly resembled the girls of our army at all. At one time we wanted to look like them with their long dresses, their clenched-fist marching style, their haughty salutes, their proud stance. But it didn't fit the Israeli temperament. So we shortened the skirt, freed the body, let the faces smile, and tipped the cap over one eye.

"You've seen my girls parade; aren't they elegant? I wanted them to keep, even as soldiers, all the charm of women. How do you say that in French—femininity?"

Two girls go past and smile at us. One of them is as plump as a quail and as blonde as wheat, the other dark-haired and slender. The first must have come from Poland or Rumania, the other from Iraq or Yemen.

Colonel Levy continues: "After the British army, my life was with the Haganah: the underground struggle, the ships that unloaded by night their cargos of death-camp survivors whom the British wanted to turn back; the bombs too, the firing squads, the attacks on the kibbutzim and on our convoys, which blew up on the roads.

"I sometimes have to remind these young ones that we didn't receive our independence on a silver platter."

Stella Levy was the first woman officer in the Haganah and then, after the war of independence, in the Tsahal. It was she who was charged with creating the women's army.

She continues her inspection of the camp, pinching chubby cheeks as Napoleon pinched the ears of his "old guardsmen." Suddenly she frowns and dryly gives an order to her captain-adjutant, a phlegmatic Rumanian, then smiles again: "Paradoxically," she goes on, "it is when she is mobilized that *the Israeli woman is liberated and emancipated completely. She leaves the family nest, and from the cocoon comes a butterfly. She is metamorphosed, and in the communal life she acquires a sense of her responsibilities. She matures during her military service. She arrives a girl and leaves a grown-up woman—and an Israeli woman, no longer a Tunisian, a German, or a Yemenite.*

"In Israel, you see, military service is, for women, an apprenticeship for their future lives. They meet boys whom they could never have gotten to know otherwise and enjoy the freedom of comradeship with them. It is in the army that they usually find their happiness, because they can make a choice."

Colonel Levy leads me into a barracks where some student officers are undergoing a weapons inspection: The contents of packs are spread out and their submachine guns disassembled on the beds. Sergeants-major of the opposite sex are carrying out the inspection. Nothing escapes them—a speck of dust, a tiny spot of rust on a weapon, a loose button.

Standing at the feet of their beds, the young girls watch anxiously as the "masters" look with disgust down the barrels of their submachine guns. They are of all types and of all races. Some are very beautiful, and all are glowing with health.

Once we are out of the barracks, Colonel Levy explains: "This period in the army will permit a whole generation of girls who came from completely different countries to transform themselves through contact with one another. We shall turn them into modern Israelis, active, courageous, self-reliant, free of anachronistic prohibitions, who must nonetheless perform a number of difficult duties."

Once again, we pass the grillwork that separates the men's camp from the women's. A short detour of fifty yards is all it takes to go around it. I ask, "Doesn't the presence of boys and girls in the same camp lead to——?"

She brushes the objection aside with a sweeping gesture.

"There are imbeciles who have said that the Israeli army is a brothel. Not only the Arabs, not only our good Israeli Ortho-dox Jews, but also the Jews of New York and London. Let's be serious. We're no longer in the Middle Ages. Incessantly watching over a young girl won't prevent her from taking a lover if she wants to.

"In Israel boys and girls are brought up together from infancy. This common living goes even further in the kib-butzim. And relations between boys and girls are neither better nor worse in the army than in civilian life. The girls spend five weeks in this training camp you are visiting. They are then transferred, according to their specialties, into dif-ferent services. But we make sure that they do their time in the city where their parents live. They can thus go back home every evening.

"Although enjoying a special independent status, the women's corps has its permanent units, which belong to the active army. We train our officers and noncoms in this same camp. Although the recruits stay only five weeks, the student noncoms stay here three months longer. Then they either become instructors themselves or take officer's training. They must then pass a more thorough examination before a sort of jury, which questions them on all sorts of matters before authorizing them to take the next six-month training phase. The women soldiers you see marching in parades do not belong to any particular unit. They are simply students in the officers' and noncoms' schools. It's from among the re-servists, the ones who volunteer, of course, that the perma-nent cadres are recruited.

"Then they reenlist for a period of one to three years. Of course, they can then marry and have children. When they are pregnant they continue to work until the seventh month; they have the right to a special uniform. After this, they have three months' leave with pay, and, if they live, a year's leave without pay."

"But they never come back?"

"*Almost always. During the Six-Day War my office was converted into a regular nursery. My adjutants, whose husbands had been mobilized and whose parents were too far away, didn't know what to do with their children, and so they brought them along.*

"*For us, the army's first job is to create in a woman the sense of being necessary to the defense of her country. We don't want her to be excluded from this thrilling adventure of creating a new nation. We insist that she take part in it just like a man, and with the same rights.*"

As we enter the barracks that serves as a mess hall, I stand back to let Colonel Levy's captain-adjutant pass through the door ahead of me. She stops for a moment, turns to me, and, in a very pure French with a slight Rumanian accent, thanks me.

"*We aren't accustomed, you know, to this kind of politeness. In Israel, the man shoves the woman aside to go ahead of her. She is his equal.*"

She sighs: "*A little less equality, a little more consideration.*"

THE GADNA

Another striking feature of the Israeli army is the intimacy that exists among soldiers, noncoms, and officers. Everyone seems to know everyone else very well, to belong to the same family. This phenomenon arises partly from the premilitary education of every young soldier, an organization known as the Gadna.

The young Israeli can be born in a kibbutz, a moshav, or a city—in Jerusalem, Tel Aviv, or Haifa. The Israeli soldier is invariably born in the bosom of the Gadna youth battalions.

Privates, like career and reserve officers, have all passed through the Gadna. Military preparation is an integral part of the educational system. It is obligatory like all the other subjects. This is understandable in a country that owes its existence entirely to the high quality of its army. Military preparation for both boys and girls takes place within the ranks of the youth battalions. But the Gadna has other aims besides simply teaching kids how to fire rifles or get through barbed wire. It has loftier ambitions: to form, from childhood, the future Israeli soldier.

Its emblem is a lozenge on a green background, marked with a bow and arrow. It reminds one of the insignia of a scout or trailblazer. But that is certainly its only point of resemblance to those movements. One of its chiefs told me, while we were visiting a base tucked in a stand of eucalyptus trees:

"The Gadna's mission is to make youngsters understand that they must defend the security of their country and guard it constantly. For many of them it is a brand-new idea, at least for those who were not born in Israel and come from the Arab countries of the Middle East or the Maghreb. The army represents in their eyes only a system of oppression. It was the army that hunted them down in Egypt and Iraq. They have a horror of it. It isn't easy to change their attitude, even though they know that the Israeli army at last is their own. They still have some reflex suspicions and fear, of which we must cure them. We seek in particular to develop energy and a taste for the communal life in young people. We teach them to sing while marching and we teach them to dance the horah (a sort of Israeli circle dance). We teach them to know their country by traveling it on foot, and we present its history on the very spots where it occurred. We want them to know that they will be the defenders of a country that is constantly under threat."

The Gadna is a military organ directly attached to the army, administered by it, and commanded by officers seconded to it. Like the army, the Gadna is apolitical. The army is always on the move. Soldiers march hundreds of miles across the country. The instructors take advantage of this to teach the history of the areas that they cross, from biblical times to the modern era, as well as their geography and ethnography, their own flora and fauna.

Marches of this kind, combining practical training with history and geography lessons, begin in the Gadna. When the young Israeli has completed his four years in the Gadna and his three years in the army, he cannot help but know his country.

In the base I visited, instructors—a woman for the boys and a man for the girls—were teaching kids fourteen to seventeen years old how to take a rifle apart and how to get through, around, and over obstacles. I sought an explanation of what seemed to me an anomaly and was told that it is a matter of psychology: A boy will not want to seem lacking in courage if his leader is a woman, and vice versa. The Gadna has fourteen-year-old children living on a military base in accordance with military routine. Are we in Sparta?

"Between Sparta and Israel there is the same difference as that between a love of warfare and the hard necessity of self-defense—even though both produce indifference to danger" (Paul Ginievski, *Bouclier*).

The Gadna was founded in 1948 by the Haganah, and its youth units fought against the Arab Legion in Jerusalem. The three great commandments that ruled the secret army of the Haganah at that time were to know why one was fighting, to know the people at whose sides one was fighting and to live with them as comrades without any distinction of class or rank, and to know Israel "with one's feet." The program of the Gadna implements this philosophy with marches across Israel (including pursuits, tracking games, and night excursions throughout the country and along all the frontiers); foot races and obstacle races; judo; fighting with staffs (inspired by the Bedouin, whose main weapon is the shepherd's staff); rifle shooting (the Gadnaim have several times taken first prize in marksmanship in the annual nationwide competitions, in which the best marksmen of all the army units compete); and grenade throwing.

The Gadna takes two different forms. In all the secondary schools, in city and country, it is an obligatory service for young people fourteen to eighteen years old, regardless of sex. This service lasts four years. During the first year it is limited to one hour of instruction daily and one full day of training every month. At the end the youngsters are sent to a camp for six days, or else they go on a long march in a group. In the second year the program is the same, but the stay at camp is extended to eleven days.

In the third year the youngsters spend fourteen days in an agricultural colony. One such camp is located at Beer Ora, six miles north of Elath in the heart of the desert. A year ago the Jordanian frontier was less than three miles away and the Egyptian frontier of the Sinai six miles. Today the Jordanian frontier is still in the same place, but the Egyptian frontier has been pushed back considerably, to the Gulf of Suez, 125 miles away.

It isn't exactly a village but a "living spot," as they say in Hebrew: a green oasis in a lunar landscape. It consists of wooden barracks and some tents that come partly from American surplus stocks in Europe. They are yellow, covered with dust, patched in places, and twenty years old. Nearby are a chicken coop, which provides eggs for Elath; a turkey run; a stable; some palm trees; and many fig trees. This whole community is sustained by a pipeline, which brings irrigation water from far away. It is a farm in the middle of the desert, operated by young Gadna members who come in relays every two weeks.

The young people of the agricultural schools operated by the Alijat Hanoar (the educational department for young orphan immigrants), who are destined for the Nahal and kibbutz life, stay twenty-one days instead of fourteen.

During the first term of the fourth year the young people undergo six days of intensive training in preparation for transfer into the army.

During these four years the instructors have plenty of

time to study and assess their Gadna charges; in fact, when the young people enter the Tsahal each is preceded by a personal dossier that will subsequently be completed by the army's psychological services. There are no unknown soldiers in the Israeli armed forces.

The second form the Gadna takes is that of a "voluntary service" for young apprentices who no longer go to school. Agreements are reached between the army and their employers, by the terms of which they take part in exercises two days a month and twice more for three days each. The Gadna has more than 300 such voluntary youth clubs in the cities and towns. It is estimated that the organization reaches and leaves its mark on some 80 percent of Israeli youth between the ages of thirteen and eighteen, more than 50,000 young people.

The Gadna helped construct the road that runs along the shores of the Dead Sea between Sodom and the kibbutzim of Ein Gedi. It helped to absorb the waves of immigrants who came to Israel after 1948, and in 1955–1956 it helped to fortify the villages of the Negev against the fedayin from Egypt and the Gaza Strip. Finally, just before the war in June 1967, it converted itself into a civil-defense organ in the big cities. It thus fell to the Gadna to supervise the civilians who were digging trenches and shelters in the parks.

Quite often Gadna youths are to be seen directing traffic in the big cities—with competence and poise. According to the particular branch of the army toward which he is headed, the young Gadna member has the choice of four fields of specialization: aviation, marine, communications, and infantry.

The Gadna-Avir (aviation) trains its young members on light planes and gliders. This preparation reduces instruction to essentials and allows a choice from the start. In the Gadna-Naval, military instruction is carried so far that, once in the navy, former Gadnaim are automatically made petty officers. (As a rule, every member of the Gadna who passes an aptitude test at seventeen goes into the army at eighteen as a corporal.) A Gadna member who has put in his entire time in Gadna-Transmissions is ready to serve in combat with either the infantry or the tank corps.

I asked the instructors whether or not young people willingly accept this kind of obligatory military preparation, which is much more like being alerted for war. They told me that these young people were so happy to live together, far from their families in the great outdoors, and that they took so much pleasure in camping under tents and marching day and night that the instructors never had any problems with them.

Sparta? Perhaps, but the army carefully avoids giving these children uniforms, in order not to accentuate unduly the paramilitary side that might, for European-born parents, unfortunately recall the Hitler Youth.

PSYCHOLOGY OF THE ISRAELI SOLDIER

The Israeli army makes a fetish of secrecy and espionage. This attitude is maddening for the foreign observer—right up to the moment that he takes his part in the game and amuses himself with it. At least that's how it was for me. This fetish arises both from the army's underground origins and from that childlike and touching side of the Israelis, who are finding after 2,000 years of Diaspora that they are a people like other peoples. They raise tomatoes and grapefruit, the best in that part of the world, which are guarded by soldiers. They can't get over this miracle and unconsciously try to make it even more mysterious.

We know all the matériel of the Israeli army: the French Mirages, the British Centurions, the American Hawk missiles, the Belgian automatic rifles and Stock mortars. The Israelis have invented a few gadgets: some tank ammunition and the delayed-action bombs for destroying runways. But these devices are simply the results of brilliant tinkering.

What is truly remarkable, on the other hand, is their system of ultra-rapid mobilization, their boosting of the "productivity" of tanks and planes by using matériel to the extreme limit of its possibilities and of the soldiers too by building their endurance.

The organization of the army is not particularly original; it is adapted both to the type of warfare that the particular geography of the country demands and to the psychology of the Arab enemy. The secret of the Tsahal's worth lies in the high quality of the Israeli—in his character and in the necessities that hold him.

The motivations that drive the Israeli soldier and produce his particular behavior—that is where the secret, if there is a secret, lies. This message is clear in the Bible, in the history of the Diaspora and that of Zionism, in the founding of Israel, and in the tenacity with which an entire people has continued to survive.

An Israeli colonel, assigned to training young soldiers in total preparedness for war, explained it to me. "For the Israeli there is no choice between 'the suitcase and the coffin.' He must win—or die witnessing the destruction of everything that he and his have built and, worse still, the loss of the self-respect that they have found again through their identity as Jews in a Jewish land."

He told me the following story. It happened in 1936, when he was eight and lived in a moshav near Rishon Le Ziyyon. He was playing with a friend in a wine vat. Suddenly he heard someone shout, "The Arabs are slaughtering Jews in the vineyards!" He climbed out of the vat, to see terrified men and women running in all directions without a thought for taking up weapons and joining together to defend themselves. These people had come from Russia and Poland, where they had known pogroms, and they behaved just as if a new pogrom were taking place. "At that point," he said, "I was so ashamed that I wanted to throw up. At fourteen, I went into the Haganah and at seventeen into the Palmach, and I became a career officer."

The refusal to be afraid, linked to a whole past of persecution, is one of the keys to Israeli courage—which is why the traditional military command "Forward march!" has been replaced in the Israeli army by "Follow me!"

For the same reason, during the Sinai campaign in 1956 Moshe Dayan insisted that captains march at the heads of their companies, majors at the heads of their battalions, and colonels at the heads of their brigades. He himself, as the commanding general, set the example, even though he was threatened with prison for it by Ben-Gurion.

The Jews of Israel understood that they had to exorcise the fear that arises from the kind of anxiety that so many "intelligent and overimaginative" people suffer. Most immigrants to Israel, even the young ones, were pacifists and believers in nonviolence. It should not be forgotten that the creators of Israel had all been influenced by the humanitarian socialist of the Russian Decembrists or the Mensheviks. But they immediately found themselves face to face with a brutal dilemma: either to let themselves be butchered or to fight. And they had come to Palestine in order not to be butchered anymore.

At first they tried, in good faith, to get along with the Palestinian Arabs, endeavoring to establish contact with them. But they failed because they spoke the language of the twentieth century to men who still lived with the fanaticism of the Middle Ages. They were rejected, forced by their enemy to enter into perpetual conflict. In this way they were led to build a country always under arms—and an army. They then applied their twentieth-century technology to warfare—and went from victory to victory.

Caught in the toils of war and heroism, they could no longer escape it. But with their customary practicality they wanted no more tragic heroes but only conquerors—and contemporary ones at that. The biblical heroes were really too distant in time, and those of the Diaspora did not belong to them, for they rejected the Diaspora. They took as their motto: "Masada will never again fall" and inscribed on their tanks the words, "Never another Auschwitz." The sons of the wandering Jew wanted to tie themselves to the land, and like Antaeus they rediscovered in this reconquered land the strengths they had lost by leaving it. Hence those marches across Israel by all the young soldiers, who are thus chained emotionally to every pebble, every town, every ruin, every dune, and every ravine.

As the quality of the Israeli army depends entirely on the Jewish soldier, a deliberate effort is made to apportion fairly among all the units those who are intelligent and those who are not, the strong and the weak, sabras and newcomers, in order to produce a homogeneous whole. The abilities of some compensate for the weaknesses of others, so that, through a kind of osmosis, the platoon or the company becomes a close-knit group of men in which fraternity goes very far—too far, if one is concerned only with efficiency. A wounded or dead comrade is never abandoned. During the Six-Day War one could see eight soldiers giving up their lives to retrieve one corpse.

The creators of the Israeli army benefited, it is true, from extraordinary opportunities. They had at their disposal men who were generally of a high technical and intellectual level, who were all volunteers and had chosen to come to Palestine, and who knew that their backs were to the wall and that there could be no retreat.

They found against them the Arabs, with their clumsy propaganda, who, by promising for twenty years to wipe out the Jews, contrived to toughen them and to rob them of all illusions about the possibility of a peace, other than one imposed by force of arms.

Colonel Shmuel told me at El Quneitra: "We now have a home; before we had nothing to defend. That's why we fight well. I don't believe in the Jewish race—no pure race exists any longer—but there is, once again, a Jewish people, and it is only here in Israel that it has a real home. What has kept us together has been not so much the Hebrew religion as the myth of the return to the Promised Land. And here we are returned, and never again will we be driven out. We would all have to be killed first, and we are determined not to let that happen."

In peacetime the Israelis adore intrigue and politics, to which they bring all the subtleties and ambiguities of Talmudic scholars. They tear each other to pieces without pity, in fact with devilish delight. But the Arab countries watch over them. They are, without wanting to be, Israel's guardian angels. The instant that they start threatening "Slaughter! Slaughter!" the profound solidarity of a people consecrated to a single relentless destiny is created anew before them.

This closing of ranks is always centered around the army, which is scrupulously kept out of politics. Then it becomes no longer merely an army. Suddenly it encompasses the whole nation, an Israel rid of defects and weaknesses. Meanwhile the Arabs continue to fight among themselves and to betray one another, even during the "holy war"—a term that has lost all meaning through being proclaimed too often.

General Ali Azar told me that he had found documents on the Golan Heights proving that the Syrian secret service had been far busier spying on the Soviet advisers, even in the midst of war, than on the movements of Israeli troops.

General S.L.A. Marshall, a military expert who has written a number of works, sums up, in *Sinai Victory,* the central principles of Israeli tactics:

To command means to betake oneself to the point of greatest danger.
There are no excuses for staying behind. When no order has been received, imagine what the order would be.
In case of doubt, strike. The shortcut to security is the road to the enemy's hill.
Do not attack head-on; there is usually a better approach.
If you do attack head-on, arrange things so that you don't present a broad target.
When the troops are really exhausted, stop and let them rest.

Do not put off combat for want of provisions; provisions are
probably on the way to you.
When you are caught in enemy fire it is better to move than to
dig in.
When you attack, dare, dare, dare.

These are the tactics of commando units, whose worth depends entirely on the quality and determination of men.

In this book I have not spoken at all of either the infantry
or the navy. The infantry is in almost all respects exactly like
the paratroops. Except for the jumping, its training is based
on the same principles. I shall give just one example: In the
battle for the Golan Heights, out of 800 men in one infantry
battalion 400 were volunteers. Caught in a murderous mortar
barrage during the approach, fifteen officers and noncoms
and fifty enlisted men were killed; eighty men were wounded.
But, commanded by privates, the survivors refused reinforcements and captured the position.

The navy, which distinguished itself in 1948 by using old
tubs that leaked on all sides to smuggle hundreds of thousands of concentration-camp survivors into Israel, can play
only a secondary role today because of the small number of
ships at its disposal.

The navy is a costly service, and Israel's budget has a
permanent deficit. Because the navy is less essential to the
defense of Israel than are aircraft and tanks, it is sacrificed
to them. For this reason, I confess, I am not at all interested
in it. But I am convinced that the Israeli sailor is as good at
his job as are the other soldiers of the other armed forces.

Not being a fortuneteller, I cannot foresee what the future
of Israel will be. But I can at least say this much: As long as
the Israeli army is distinguished by men possessing such
moral strength and technical brillance, Israel is not likely to
be defeated or destroyed. As long as it has to face only politically and economically unstable Arab countries, however
well-armed they may be by their Soviet allies (let's hope,

however, that the latter are never mad enough to furnish them with atomic arms), Israel is not likely to be defeated or destroyed.

Even if one doesn't believe in God, it is unthinkable for a man of our century to imagine for a moment that the "sons of the miracle" could be driven from their Promised Land. Then it would be necessary to refuse to believe in miracles, and life would no longer be bearable.

Appendix A.
The Jewish Military Spirit in the Bible

During the Six-Day War some fundamental traits of the Israeli military spirit were revealed in an unmistakable manner: the taste for sudden, swift attack, prefaced by extremely thorough technical preparation combined with perfect secrecy. The military operations of the Tsahal are always prepared in the greatest secrecy, with the most precise knowledge of the enemy's resources and means—which is why the basic forms of warfare as waged by the Israelis are the ambuscade and, especially, the lightning raid. We find these tactics already in the Bible. On occasion, Israeli military men and historians like to refer to their ancestors' feats of arms and to emphasize their own army's affinity with their ancient exploits. Here are two examples taken from the holy book.

GIDEON'S CAMPAIGN AGAINST THE MIDIANITES

One decisive campaign was that conducted by Gideon in the eastern part of the valley of Jezreel against the Midianites from east of the Jordan. It is described in minute detail in the Bible (*Judges* 6–8). The operation was composed of three phases: recruiting, preparing, and planning the campaign; the battle and its characteristic features; and pursuit of the enemy.

The first phase bore witness to the popular character of the Jewish army and its tribal organization. The recruiting was certainly not unrelated to the character of the enemy and to the so-called "battle plan."

The plan called for few men, but they had to be properly trained. First, 10,000 men were selected out of the 32,000 who assembled in response to Gideon's call, and then, of those 10,000, the very best 300 were picked. Gideon's campaign plan was based on his understanding of the terrain, on his estimate of his own forces, and, above all, on his knowledge of the Midianites. The latter came from the east, from the other side of the Jordan. Their main weakness, in time of war, arose from the fact that they bivouacked in huge, noisy camps that could easily be attacked by surprise. A reconnaissance mission led by Gideon himself preceded his final decision.

Gideon deployed the bulk of his forces along the Jordan to block a potential Midianite retreat. He divided his 300 elite troops into three companies of 100 men each; nowadays, we would say into three commando groups. To each man he gave a trumpet and a torch placed in a jug—two rather unconventional weapons, perhaps, but perfectly adapted to the circumstances. Trumpet blasts were supposed to cause confusion in the enemy encampment, and the torches were destined to destroy the fortifications, in this instance the tents that sheltered men, women, and children. Because surprise had to be total, Gideon ordered that the torches be carried inside the jugs until the very last moment.

The hour of the attack was also carefully chosen: the middle of the night, when sleep enveloped the camp, after the changing of the guard but just before the eyes of the new sentinels could become adjusted to the darkness. In such an operation the coordination of all the elements had to be absolutely perfect. For this reason Gideon decided to give the signal to attack personally.

In the second phase of the plan, the three companies of 100 men took up stations to the north, west, and south of the enemy camp, purposely leaving the fourth side of the camp open to encourage the enemy's eventual flight to the east. On that side the Israelite forces that were not taking part in the attack were waiting for them. It is not hard to imagine the panic that must have seized the Midianites and the sound of the trumpets, accompanied by the smashing of the jugs and the war cry "the sword of God and Gideon!" followed soon by the conflagration of the tents.

In a third phase, Gideon undertook relentless pursuit of the enemy as far as the Jordan, where his other warriors were waiting to bar the way. He crossed the Jordan to the east bank and finally took the kings Zebah and Zalmunna prisoner. The battle was decisive: It followed a perfect plan perfectly executed.

In the *Book of Judges* Gideon stands out as an original and courageous military leader who knew how to exploit the element of surprise and the aggressive spirit to the maximum. His exploits underline this primary military truth: that what is important in battles is not really the size or power of an army but its fighting spirit and the possibility of injecting the greatest surprise into the choice of time, place, method, and weapons of the conflict.

DAVID AND THE AMMONITES

One of the most famous battles fought by the armies of David as described in 2 *Samuel*, 10–11, is the one that Joab led against Hanun, King of the Ammonites. Joab, his regular army, and his mercenaries had earlier been surprised by the Syrians (who had come to lend a hand to the Ammonites) and had been beaten by the combined armies. But Joab had saved his men from total extermination by his brilliant command, his quick decisions, and his fighting spirit. He proceeded to divide his men into two equal parts, sending one against the Ammonites, and himself leading the other against the Syrians. This counterattack is reminiscent of that of

Rameses II when the Pharaoh found himself pinned between enemy armies at the battle of Kadesh. And again, as at Kadesh, the fighting ended without a victory—that is, without the capture of Rabbah.

David appears to have learned three things from that earlier engagement: that he had little chance thenceforward of beating the Ammonites without first knocking out the Syrians; that in this sort of action Rabbah should be approached from the north rather than the south; and that the regular army alone was not sufficient to fight such a battle and required the help of all the militia forces as well. In a subsequent battle, which took place north of Rabbah near Succoth, David assembled the whole people of Israel and inflicted a crushing defeat on the Syrians led by Shobach. But it is clear that this battle was only an essential first step toward defeating and subjugating the Ammonites. After their own defeat the Syrians were afraid to help the sons of Ammon.

This battle has long been considered one of the most decisive of that period and almost as important for the Jews as the duel between David and Goliath. Remembering his earlier defeat, David fielded against the Ammonites not only Joab and the regular army but also once again the entire people of Israel—and with them his decisive weapon, the "sacred ark." Most of the details of this campaign are related to use by Uriah the Hittite. It was a difficult campaign and the Jews suffered some reverses before carrying off the final victory. It was in one of these episodes that Uriah, sent to the front by Joab, was killed.

Appendix B.

1948-1968:
Israel and its Frontiers

While Palestine was still under British mandate, shortly before the birth of the State of Israel was proclaimed, the territories occupied by the Jews were limited to a narrow strip of land along the sea, from St. John of Acre to south of Jaffa. This strip was nowhere more than ten or twelve miles wide.

Arab detachments held upper Galilee and elements of the Haganah had an enclave along the Dead Sea southeast of Jericho. The British still occupied Haifa and the neighboring airfields. In Jerusalem, the New Town, occupied exclusively by the Jews, was besieged on three sides by the Arabs. An umbilical cord connected it with the rest of the country. This was the Bal al-Oued road.

Eight hours before the end of the British Mandate, Ben-Gurion proclaimed the State of Israel. Five Arab armies attacked. Instantly an Israeli army (the Haganah) emerged from the shadows, and even before its official existence it began to win its first victories. The new state was recognized almost simultaneously by the United States and the U.S.S.R.

On May 20 the Arab forces controlled approximately the territory set apart for them in the U.N. partition plan. It was at this moment that a cease-fire was ordered.

U.N. mediator Count Folke Bernadotte proposed a new partition plan, which called for the internationalization of

Jerusalem and the occupation of the Negev by Emir Abdullah's Arab Legion. Bernadotte was assassinated by terrorists of the Stern Gang. Israeli commandos penetrated into the Negev.

On January 6, 1949, the Egyptians asked for an armistice. The new territory of Israel had increased considerably (20 percent more than under the U.N. partition plan). It included the Negev and Galilee, but Jerusalem had not been completely occupied: The Old City and the holy places remained in Arab hands. Israel could still communicate with it only by way of a narrow corridor across Jordanian territory. On February 24, 1949, an armistice agreement was signed at Rhodes. It confirmed Israel's victory but did not recognize its new frontiers.

In 1951, fighting broke out again between Syrians and Israelis in the demilitarized zone of Lake Tiberias. Egypt forbade the passage of Israeli shipping in the Suez Canal, and a freighter was seized at Port Said.

In October 1953 the first Arab terrorist raids took place; they were answered by Israeli commando raids. For example, following the murders of a woman and two children in a kibbutz on the Jordanian frontier, the Israeli army annihilated the Jordanian village of Kibry. This attack left forty civilians dead. From that time on terrorism never ceased, nor did the reprisals.

The raids of the fedayeen caused 137 deaths in 1951, 147 in 1952, 162 in 1953, 180 in 1954, 258 in 1955 (figures supplied by Ben-Gurion).

On April 11, 1956, the Egyptian minister Hassan el Baquri declared, "I do not see why the fedayin, who hate their enemies, do not penetrate deeper into Israel and make the lives of her inhabitants a hell on earth."

On March 19, 1954, eleven Israelis were killed in the Negev during an automobile attack. Ten days later a reprisal raid was staged against the village of Nahaleen.

Nasser nationalized the Suez Canal on October 29. The

Sinai campaign began. The Israeli army benefited from the Franco-British aerial umbrella and seized the whole of the Sinai in a week. But Nasser was saved by the intervention of the Russians and the Americans. The British and French troops had to be withdrawn from Egypt. The Israelis were forced to evacuate the Sinai and all the conquered territories.

In the years that followed the Arabs rearmed, with the support of the U.S.S.R., which supplied them with modern matériel like tanks and planes, while Israel called on France and less often on the United States.

In 1964 there were violent encounters between Syrians and Israelis. The Syrian secret service controlled most of the Palestinian resistance organizations, which operated, however, from Jordan.

On January 1, 1965, a Palestinian organization, al-Fatah, made its existence known by a communiqué in which it announced that its sabotage commandos were already operating throughout Israeli territory.

In 1966 there was a struggle over the waters of the Jordan. August 15 witnessed the first battle, above Lake Tiberias, between Syrian Migs of Russian manufacture and Israeli Mirages. Four Migs were shot down. On November 13 a mine exploded under an Israeli truck, and the Israeli forces launched an attack on the village of Samwa: There were 18 dead and 134 wounded on the Jordanian side, and 125 houses were destroyed. In 1967 there was another upsurge of outrages and reprisal raids: artillery skirmishes on the Syrio-Israeli frontier and Israeli raids on the suburbs of Damascus, in the course of which six Migs were shot down.

The Soviet intelligence services invented concentrations of Israeli troops on the Syrian frontier and launched the rumor of an Israeli attack in force on Damascus. The Egyptians sent tanks into the Sinai and on May 17 proclaimed a state of alert. On May 21, following an Egyptian ultimatum, the U.N. forces packed their bags. On May 22 Nasser announced the closing of the Gulf of 'Aqaba to Israeli ships.

On June 5 Israel launched the first operation: a surprise attack on the Egyptian air bases.

In five days all the Arab armies had been routed; the Israelis occupied the west bank of the Jordan, the Old City of Jerusalem, the Gaza Strip, the Sinai, and the Golan Heights. The territory of Israel had tripled in a week.

Appendix C.

Al-Fatah and the Palestinian Resistance Movements

The movements of resistance and armed struggle that are being organized among the Palestinian refugee population, camps or dispersed throughout the various Arab countries, are not at all unified. There are twelve or thirteen of them, which have hardly any common denominator other than the struggles against Israel and the reestablishments of the Palestinian people's right to recover its lands and to live. Apart from this common desire, considerable differences exist.

These movements are, on the whole, of recent origin. For years, the "liberation" of Palestine was regarded as the prerogative not of Palestinians alone but of *all* the Arabs. The most official of the Palestinian movements was—at least until the Six-Day War—the P.L.O., or Palestine Liberation Organization. Long headed by Ahmed Shukhairy, the P.L.O. is a pure creation of the Arab League. Recognized and supported by all the member countries of that league, it is, in fact, controlled by Egypt. Before the Six-Day War its army, the P.L.A., or Palestine Liberation Army, had at its disposal eight training camps in the Gaza Strip; there were others in Egypt proper, Iraq, Jordan, Syria, and Kuwait. The active members of this army amounted to about 15,000 men. Its battalions were integrated into the various Arab armies and were responsible to both the commands of these armies and to a paralyzing Palestinian bureaucracy. In 1966 one of the members of the action committee of the P.L.O., Shatik al-Hout, leader of the Palestinian section of the Arab Nationalist Movements, the A.N.M., founded within the P.L.O. a commando organization, the Heroes of the Counterattack, whose first terrorist raids on Israeli soil were staged in October, 1966. Since the dismissal of Shukhairy in December 1967 and his replacement by Yahia Nammouda, the P.L.O., after having tried in vain to constitute itself as a conventional army, has tended to employ guerilla methods and tactics and to preach union with the other Palestinian resistance movements.

Another important movement is the Palestinian Liberation Front (Jabhat al-Fakhrir al-Falastina). This movement is more developed ideologically than is the P.L.O.: It exhorts the Palestinians to fight their own fight without becoming the pawns of "brother" Arab countries. It began as an officers' movement, then established itself as a political party in 1964, and in 1966 and 1967 entered into guerilla activities. Its most notable figure is Captain Ahmed Jibril, a former Syrian army officer, an expert in sabotage, and currently in charge of operations for the movement. The military and political level of the members of the Palestinian Liberation Front is also higher than that of the members of the P.L.O. The organization is notable for having sabotaged the Jerusalem railway. In November 1967 the Palestine Liberation Front and the Heroes of the Counterattack, which had merged before the Six-Day War, founded the P.F.L.P., the Popular Front for the Liberation of Palestine. This movement, linked to the A.N.M., whose leader Georges Hebache is currently in prison in Syria, is represented on the Palestinian National Council and keeps its membership (20 percent of that of al-Fatah) a jealously guarded secret. The people of western Jordan learned of the creation of the P.F.L.P. on November 12, 1967, when tracts urging them not to collaborate with the Israelis were distributed. On November 29, the anniversary of the U.N. resolution on the partition of Palestine, the P.F.L.P. shelled one of the districts of Petah-Tiqwa in Israel proper with mortars, clearly showing by this act that it did not intend to limit its objectives to western Jordan alone. The P.F.L.P. also has to its credit a raid on Lydda airport on December 11, 1967, and, more recently, the highjacking to Algeria on July 23, 1968, of an El Al airliner.

But all these groups, whatever their exploits or their official character, are at present eclipsed by another resistance organization, already quite old, which did not reveal its real strength until the Six-Day War: al-Fatah. Since then, the attacks, lightning raids, and ambushes on the Jordan or in the Negev have usually been the work of al-Fatah and not of the P.L.O. or the P.F.L.P.

Al-Fatah means "conquest" in Arabic. Its troops call themselves al-Assifah, "the storm."

BIRTH AND DEVELOPMENT OF AL-FATAH

Al-Fatah was born in 1956 during the temporary occupation of the Gaza Strip by the Israelis. Disgusted by the indifference and passivity of the leaders of the Arab countries, some young Palestinians launched a clandestine movement led exclusively by Palestinians and spread its slogan, "Palestine for the Palestinians" through the refugee camps. The most remarkable of its leaders—today the official spokesman of the movement—is an engineer, Yassir Arafat, also known by the name Abu Amar. Born in 1929 in Jerusalem, Arafat served in 1947–1948 in the ranks of the Palestinian militia, which tried to defend the Arab towns and villages against the assaults of the Haganah and the Irgun. After the defeat he studied engineering and became president of the Federation of Palestinian Students in 1957. As head of the alumni federation he promoted continuous contact among all the former Palestinian university students throughout the Arab world.

After the evacuation of Gaza, the Palestinian émigrés, mostly workers, who had taken part in the activities of clandestine cells came together again in 1960 in Kuwait, where they enjoyed complete freedom to organize and agitate. To swell the organization's ranks, Arafat secured the cooperation of a Palestinian journalist, Toufik Houri, who in 1958 had founded in Beirut a newspaper called *Falastinana* (*Our Palestine*). *Falastinana* became the movement's official organ and from time to time published a supplement entitled *al-Assifah* (*The Storm*), devoted to the actions of the commandos.

Yassir Arafat and his friends then founded chapters of al-Fatah in several countries, notably Kuwait, West Germany (where many Palestinians live), and Syria. The Kuwait chapter was headed by Yihia Ghavani and brought together numerous Palestinian workers; the German chapter was led by Hani al-Hassan; that of Damascus was led by a young militant, Halil al-Wazir, who was also in charge of the different sections of the organization. Once this preparatory work was finished, the first operations against Israel were unleashed at the beginning of 1965. On January 8 al-Fatah men mined El Batout dam, and leaflets distributed in Damascus and Beirut declared that "the purpose of the acts of terrorism is to transfer the Palestinian Arab nation from a group of embittered and unorganized refugees into a fighting people, acting in its own way and in its own interests." Between January and June of 1965 al-Fatah claimed no fewer than 113 sabotage operations in Israel. All these operations were conducted from the territory of the neighboring Arab countries, which were consequently put in a delicate situation vis-à-vis Israel. The popularity of al-Fatah, on the other hand, soared. In July 1966, four operations conducted from Syria were followed by an Israeli reprisal raid. On September 11, 1966, Israeli Chief of Staff General Rabin, declared that "the Syrians are the spiritual fathers of the al-Fatah group," and, following this thinly veiled threat, on November 13, 1966, Israel made a reprisal on Samwa.

The Six-Day War unquestionably marked a turning point in the career of al-Fatah. Whereas the P.L.O. was paralyzed by internal dissension and the collapse of the Arab armies, al-Fatah, starting in the summer of 1967, multiplied its incursions into Israeli-occupied territory and appreciably stepped up its guerilla activities. The situation of Palestinian resistance had changed fundamentally: Previously, guerrilla actions had been only one among several ways to weaken Israel; now they became the fundamental tactic that was to drive Israel sooner or later to evacuate the occupied territories and to negotiate with Arab intermediaries.

Guerilla activities thus increased in numbers and intensity. On July 19, 1967, there was sabotage at Tulkarem in Samaria, on July 26 fighting in Gaza and Nablus, on August 27 an ambush on the road to Jericho. Mining operations and mortar barrages were continuous; despite heavy losses, al-Fatah cadres infiltrated western Jordan and stockpiled immense quantities of weapons there. Encounters occurred most frequently in the valley of Baisa and at 'Aqaba. In November 1967 al-Fatah set up a training camp at Kuraiyima and began to strengthen its ties with the other organizations. A common military command was created within the Palestinian Council of 100 members: Al-Fatah had thirty-eight representatives, the P.L.O. thirty, the P.L.A. twenty, the P.F.L.P. ten, and all the others together two.

In 1968 fighting became a daily occurrence at Hebron, on the Golan Heights, at Baisa, at Manara, in Judea, and so on. More than thirty-seven acts of sabotage were perpetrated in one three-week period. According to General Dayan (in a press conference on March 18, 1968), the Israeli forces had killed ninety Palestinians and imprisoned 1,500 since the cease-fire in June 1967. Between February 16 and March 18 al-Fatah had committed thirty-five raids. During this time nearly fifty terrorists had been killed in the course of encounters with Israeli patrols.

Al-Fatah activity became so heavy that the Israeli army,

in order to assure the security of the military parade it planned to stage in Jerusalem, at dawn of March 21 launched a massive raid on Kuraiyima, the main base of al-Fatah and the P.F.L.P. in the region. About 1,000 men were stationed in nine camps, four auxiliary camps, two underground command posts, a provisioning base, and a large training center. The Jordanian army, which occupied the crests of the hills around Kuraiyima, lent active assistance to the Palestinian organizations while leaving them complete freedom of movement and action. The Israelis threw almost 15,000 men against the base, with tanks, armored cars, and aircraft. Despite the disproportion of forces, the battle was fierce; and, although the Palestinians' losses were heavy (more than 170 dead; according to the Israeli colonel who commanded the operation, there were 300 dead and 160 captured), they gained considerable prestige: More than 100,000 Jordanians paraded behind coffins the following day. Their recruiting offices were besieged with young men wanting to join up, and money flowed in from all the Arab capitals.

For the first time Palestinian commandos had fought side by side with soldiers of the Arab Legion against the Israelis. "The fedayeen," said one of their spokesmen, "paid in blood for their formal recognition by Jordan and even, in a certain sense, by the other Arab states." This sentiment was echoed by the words of King Hussein after the battle of Kuraiyima: "One day we may all become fedayeen."

The destruction of that base (which cost the Israelis twenty-five lives) obviously did not put an end to the activities of al-Fatah. Attacks continued with the same frequency. On August 4, 1968, in the wake of a series of particularly violent skirmishes, including one that resulted in the death of an Israeli colonel, Israeli aircraft conducted a big reprisal operation against the Palestinian commando camps in the region of Salt, a town twenty miles from Amman. For more than three hours the Israeli planes pounded al-Fatah headquarters, two big training camps, and a dozen bases. Again the Palestinian losses were very heavy (twenty-eight men killed and eighty-two wounded).

STRUCTURE OF AL-FATAH

The members of al-Fatah, whether the leaders or the guerillas themselves, take refuge in absolute anonymity and keep their identities and numbers scrupulously secret. It is commonly admitted that they number between 7,000 and 10,000 men, al-Fatah having absorbed a good proportion of the troops of the P.L.O. All the same, the movement's forces are quite distinct from those of the P.L.O., who once aspired to organize themselves as a conventional army; al-Fatah, on the other hand, is a clandestine and revolutionary movement, patterned on the model of the Algerian F.L.N. or the Vietcong. To belong to al-Fatah, a man must first of all not belong to any of the political parties that exist in the Arab countries. In joining the movement, a fighter must sever all his former organizational ties. Even so, the political leadership of al-Fatah appears to harbor several different tendencies, which it is not for the moment seeking to unify: former Baathists (the Baath is the Arab socialist party, in power in Syria and Iraq), liberal Moslems, Marxists, members of the Moslem Brotherhood, and some Arab nationalists.

The militants and fighters of al-Fatah are 99 percent Palestinians, recruited mainly from the Palestinian communities scattered throughout the Arab countries or the rest of the world. Founded by students and intellectuals at the University of Cairo, al-Fatah has kept its student nucleus, swollen by volunteers from all the Arab capitals, as well as from abroad: from Germany (where there are 20,000 Palestinians —3,000 students and 17,000 workers), from Switzerland, from France, and from the United States. In its ranks are engineers, doctors, lawyers, and a few peasants. The average age is very revealing: It is between twenty-five and thirty, and the majority of the members were born in exile or left

Palestine at the age of four or five. The presence of so many students and intellectuals, trained mostly by Algerian instructors, gives al-Fatah a very special character, closer to that of the Algerian F.L.N. than to the P.L.O. The example of Ahmed Archid, who was arrested by the Israelis in 1967, attests to this character. He was secretary of the Palestinian student chapter in Karlsruhe, Germany, where he had been studying industrial economy since 1960. He enlisted in the ranks of al-Fatah in 1965 and founded, in Germany, cells of militants with three or four members each, all under a single command. After the Six-Day War he took a three-week training course at Blida in Algeria with about 120 other students. On August 20, 1967, he was sent to Syria and became administrative officer of al-Fatah command in the Jenin sector, where he was later taken prisoner. Then there is Abdel Fattah Issa Hammoud, another student. Born in 1933, he lived in Gaza from 1948 on, studied at the University of Cairo, took his engineering degree, and then worked on the Persian Gulf and in Saudi Arabia. He abandoned his career and his profession for the armed struggle: "I am thirty-five years old, but I am newborn," he wrote to a friend. He was killed in action on March 28, 1968.

The troops of al-Fatah are led by military commands located for the most part in Judea, Samaria, and Galilee. These commands are composed of political committees and military officers. Each combat unit has, on the average, fifteen men, a military chief, and a political commissar charged with securing the withdrawal and, more important, politically educating the rural and urban masses. Recruiting members for commando groups takes place, as we have seen, among students and peasants, while local notables and the *petit bourgeois* tend instead to "collaborate" with the Israeli occupying forces.

The principal al-Fatah commando bases are at present in Jordan, or, more precisely, Trans-Jordan; the Syrian bases have been dismantled or abandoned since the Six-Day War.

There are also numerous "movable bases" in western Jordan but as yet no permanent ones. Although al-Fatah is quite important in rural areas, it has hardly taken root in the cities.

The main base is still Kuraiyima, which was reoccupied after the Israeli raid. According to the Israeli intelligence services, other bases of lesser importance exist at Ghor Safi, Chouna, Tel Arbain, El Mafraq, Suweilih, and El Hamra, as well as at Salt. The lightning operations conducted by the Israeli army regularly manage—but only for very limited periods—to neutralize these bases.

The guerillas also pursue their training in Syria and Algeria, as well as in Cuba, the United Arab Republic and even in Red China. Algeria undertakes the training of numerous Palestinians at Blida and also at a base in Syria. Al-Fatah has military matériel that is more and more modern, coming from China (which equips al-Fatah troops directly), Russia, Czechoslovakia, and even the United States. It also has weapons seized from the enemy in various encounters. After having used mines for a long time, al-Fatah now increasingly employs mortars, bazookas (as in the attack on the house of the lawyer Farouki in Jerusalem on December 30, 1967), and even missiles (as in the destruction of the pipe lines in January 1968). Members of al-Fatah often stress the fact that they do not depend exclusively on Arab sources for their arms, as the P.L.O. does.

The organization is financed by collections taken up among Palestinians in exile—students and intellectuals, who are in touch with their families in refugee camps, or oil workers in the emirates of the Persian Gulf, who give the movement 5 percent of their pay (not to mention certain Palestinian "millionaires" who aid the movement, as a representative of al-Fatah put it, "to ease their consciences").

TRAINING

Whether it takes place in Trans-Jordan or abroad, the training of al-Fatah commandos is very rigorous. First of all, they are taught the most elementary skills: how to cross a river like the Jordan with submachine guns on their backs, how to ready a mortar for action, knife fighting, close combat, how to rush through flames, how to jump from a roof, how to scale rocks, how to cut electrified barbed wire, and so on. This intensive training is extended not only to al-Fatah members but also to a good many of the Palestinian refugees themselves. In Jordan children ten to fourteen years old currently go through a period of instruction in guerilla tactics. Military training, in the course of which new members of al-Assifah commando groups are chosen, is inseparable from education of a political order.

Let us examine Yassir Arafat's explanation, in an interview granted to *Jeune Afrique,* of the principles of this political-military education:

When a volunteer presents himself to al-Fatah, he first goes through a probationary period in the course of which he is subjected to different tests and undergoes elementary training. He then goes back to his customary activities until such a time as he is recalled for more thorough military and ideological training. It is only after this stage that he takes part in actual engagements with the enemy as a member of an al-Fatah unit. He still returns often to his work, while remaining entirely at the movement's disposal. He pursues his training and his studies and applies himself, at the same time, to spreading among the populace the message of the armed struggle for the liberation of Palestine.

In the elite inner circle commandos must learn Hebrew and eventually try to win over to their cause the Jewish people, who are always carefully distinguished from the Israeli government itself.

COMMANDO TACTICS

In the field al-Fatah's tactics consist of surprise attacks on the Israeli occupation forces: first drawing them off by means of diversionary movements and afterward, if possible, melting into the Palestinian masses who remain in western Jordan. The guerilla fighters' watchword was for a long time "hit

and run"; today it is "hit and resist," which is why the encounters with the Israeli soldiers have become ever bloodier
and rougher. But, considering that the Israeli army is itself
extremely mobile and that the territory of western Jordan is
very narrow, the hit-and-run principle remains just as valid.

One al-Fatah commando expressed himself as follows:
"Israel can very quickly reach any point of the occupied territory, thanks to permanent helicopter surveillance, and can
also intervene quickly with armor. Our guerilla opeartions
must therefore be timed to the second: five minutes to surprise and destroy an enemy patrol, seven minutes to make
sure that there are no survivors, and five minutes to return to
base. Two minutes more could mean death."

In this struggle, conducted inside occupied Jordan but
generally from bases in Trans-Jordan, al-Fatah has encountered certain unexpected difficulties. Many members of the
commando groups, born in exile, do not know the topography
of the country. So Palestinians who left the country in 1947–
1948, at the age of twenty or twenty-five and who therefore
know the territory and local conditions very well are selected
to accompany the young ones as guides and weapons and
ammunition carriers. They stay in the towns and villages until
the operation is completed.

Al-Fatah's immediate military objective is the stepping-up
of guerilla activity within Israel and occupied Jordan. A
recent declaration (August 6, 1968) sets forth the aims of
the movement: to prevent all new immigration of Jews into
Israel, to harm the economic stability of Israel, to ruin Israel's
tourist industry, to prevent Jewish immigrants from settling
on Palestinian soil, to weaken the Israeli economy by forcing
the Tel Aviv government to devote most of its resources to
security measures, to convince Israelis that life in Israel will
be impossible in the future because of the atmosphere of
terrorism.

To deal Israel really heavy blows by sabotaging its economic foundations and stopping the influx of immigration—

two very ambitious goals—it is necessary above all to create a force capable of wresting recognition from the Palestinians, the Israelis, and the Arab countries. Only in armed struggle can this force prove its right to recognition as the sole spokesman for the Palestinian Arabs in the eyes of the Israelis. This struggle must be purely Palestinian and carried on through continuous guerilla activity, rather than through conventional warfare supported by Arab neighbors. In 1966 a controversy divided the A.N.M. and al-Fatah on this subject: The former emphasized unified strategy and assistance from the progressive Arab countries (the U.A.R., Syria, and Algeria), whereas al-Fatah wanted to launch the struggle "here and now," in fact to heat up a situation that had already lasted for sixteen years. The Six-Day War seems to have brought about the conditions necessary for the development of the guerilla warfare as preached by al-Fatah. Before the war the Palestinians were fighting from foreign territory. Since June 1967 they have finally been able to fight on home ground and to attempt to win over the people living under the occupation.

Although militarily the struggle involves harassing the Israeli forces, politically it means "destroying the racist and colonialist Zionist state, not at all its people" (Yassir Arafat). This last distinction is important: We are a long way, here, from the threats of Shukhairy. It is, however, the idea of a Jewish state reserved to Jews, where the Law of the Return reigns unchallenged, that al-Fatah wants to upset through protracted guerilla activity. It wants to force Israel to admit that it cannot continue to exist in its present form. In other words, it seeks to make Israel abandon the entire ideological content of Zionism. "Our aim," Arafat explains, "is to enable all Palestinians to go back to their country and live as Palestinians in that democracy." To liberate Palestine through the armed struggle of all the Palestinian people with only indirect assistance from the Arab world—such is the new objective. What would Palestine's social regime be after liberation? Al-Fatah does not comment on this point, although it calls, in a rather vague way, for a socialist, secular, and democratic Palestine, where Jews, Moslems, and Christians would enjoy equal rights. In any case, given the embryonic condition of the resistance movement and the lack of political maturity among the Palestinian population, all discussion on this point seems out of place to the al-Fatah leaders. It is more important, first, to make the organization known and to build up a position of strength.

THE NEW ISRAELI-PALESTINIAN WAR

The leaders of al-Fatah, in their insistence that the essential thing for them is the armed struggle and not the development of a "program" or of some political line or other, obviously have in mind the Algerian F.L.N. The F.L.N. is a perfect example of a movement that did not originate as a political party and never fought in a partisan spirit. Against all expectations, the F.L.N. was able to awaken and to develop the aspirations of an entire people after a century of assimilation. It took up arms against a big colonial power and created in Algerian blood and bones the sense of an Algerian nation. The struggle—an eight-year struggle—imposed the "fact of Algeria" on the French and converted the terrorists of 1954 into "authentic representatives of the Algerian people." The Palestinian people will become—or become again—a genuine people only through a similar test. But the basic problems of al-Fatah arise precisely from the fact that Palestine is not Algeria and that the potential of the Palestine resistance is more limited (or at least very different) from that of the Algerian resistance. By becoming specifically Palestinian and no longer Arab in its outlook, al-Fatah has undoubtedly come closer to the F.L.N. spirit. But it faces very serious problems that did not challenge the F.L.N.

The first is the problem of terrain: The Israeli and western Jordanian territories hardly offer facilities for guerilla operations; they are too narrow, and natural hiding places are few, in contrast to the terrains of Algeria and Vietnam. The climate of the Middle East permits mechanized or airborne troop actions all year round, and no part of Israel is safe from air attack. The commandos' freedom of action is thus very limited. The idea here is that "guerilla warfare is possible only in a country of big dimensions, and not in a little state like, for example, Belgium."

The second problem is relations with the local population. The people of Palestine have not, up to now, played a decisive role in the struggle against Israel. Numerically, in the Israeli and western Jordanian territories the Arab population is weaker than the Jewish population: 1 million Arabs to 2.2 million Jews, which makes the Israeli security services' task of control easier. In the occupied territories themselves, the commando groups possess only "mobile bases," which is a euphemism. The people of western Jordan do not always share the ambitions of the Arab refugees, and, in contrast to the Algerian guerillas, the fedayeen cannot feel free to move around occupied territories "like fish in the water," as could the F.L.N. and as does the Vietcong today.

The third problem is the nature of the enemy. Israel is neither France nor South Vietnam assisted by the United States. There is no question of toppling a regime or of chasing Israel out of overseas colonies not immediately vital to its existence. The terrorist aims, whether they are expressed in the murderous words of Shukhairy or in the more measured phrases of al-Fatah, threaten the very existence of Israel as a *state*. It follows that, on both sides, the struggle takes on sharpness and a different character.

UNIFICATION OF THE PALESTINIAN
RESISTANCE MOVEMENTS AND CREATION
OF PALESTINIAN NATIONAL CONSCIOUSNESS

To attain the position of strength that will enable it to surmount its present difficulties, al-Fatah will have both to unify

the different Palestinian resistance movements and to educate
the Palestinian masses politically. In its time the F.L.N. knew
how to unify the whole Algerian resistance, if necessary by
force.

In January 1968 al-Fatah organized a conference, to which
it invited all the Palestinian guerilla groups. Seven of them
responded and the eight organizations joined in three military
formations and created a common military council: the Congress of Palestinian Fedayeen, charged with cooperation and
coordination of the different movements. The first step,
though still very theoretical, had been taken toward political
and military unification. Yahia Hamouda, who had just taken
up his functions as the new head of the P.L.O., announced
that he would do everything possible to help unify the different Palestinian organizations.

Despite declarations of intention, however, al-Fatah nour-
ishes a tenacious suspicion of the P.L.O., the artificial creation
of the Arab League: "It's in fighting that the true patriots are
divided from the fake guerilla fighters. So we say, no prefabricated unity, but encounters in the field. The armed
struggle will not only cement the movement together but
will indicate our priorities to us." The P.L.O., in the view of
al-Fatah leaders, must first rid itself of the after effects of its
creation: the cult of personality (Shukhairy), a paralyzing
bureaucracy, the absence of political and military strategy,
fear of direct action. "At the outset," says Arafat, "the P.L.O.
organized its troops along the conventional lines for conventional warfare. We have always thought that that was like
wanting to run before learning to walk." But even more
essential than the unification of the resistance movements is
the formation in and through guerilla warfare of a Palestinian national consciousness. Paradoxically, the defeat of
the Arab countries in June 1967 helped—and will continue
to help—to bring this national consciousness into being. In
1947 and even in 1956 the defeat was not that of the Palestinian people but of the whole "Arab nation." For years there

was the "Arab-Israeli conflict" on one side and the "refugee problem" on the other. The Palestinians served merely as small change in a border conflict in which the "Arab world" opposed Israel and through Israel part of the Western world. There was never any question of a Palestinian state or nation that could determine its own destinies without concerning itself with the decisions of the U.N. or its "brother countries." After the 1967 defeat it became clear that the brother countries could not, and perhaps did not want to, undertake the struggle necessary to liberate Palestine. To the growing desire of the Palestinian refugees to assert their own existence against Israel was added the desire to assert themselves against the consuming but useless fraternity of the Arab countries. Therein lay al-Fatah's difficulty: to establish itself as a national movement in the eyes of the Palestinians (who are only slowly discovering their own "nationality"), the Israelis, and above all the other Arabs.

The policy that al-Fatah has adopted toward the Arab countries is, in principle, very simple: The struggle that it wages against Israel is the struggle of the entire Arab world and is basically a struggle against Western imperialism. Out of this policy comes a solidarity extending to all the avant-garde movements in the Third World. "We are an integral part of the Arab revolution to eliminate the governmental structures of Israel and to establish unity and social justice in this part of the world," Arafat declares.

But, beyond these declarations of principle, al-Fatah's dominant concern is most certainly to assert jealously its own autonomy from the other Arab nations, the various governments that dominate them, and the shifting ideologies that they profess. "From the point of view of ideology," the movement's spokesman says, "we have no organic and ideological tie with any partisan tendency in the Arab world." This attitude explains why al-Fatah requires its members to break with the parties and movements to which they have previously belonged and why it stubbornly refuses to organize itself as a political party. Al-Fatah wants to remain underground and not to intervene in the affairs of the countries in which Palestinian communities are established. It strives to win the refugees away from Jordanian, Syrian, or Lebanese domination as much as possible, for financial, as well as for military, reasons. Such independence is virtually a fact in Jordan and Lebanon; it is much more problematic in the U.A.R. and Syria.

The attitude of the Arab governments, with the exception of Algeria, remains very ambiguous. It is impossible for the leaders of the U.A.R., Syria, Jordan, and Lebanon not to support the actions of the Palestinian commandos, at least verbally. The pressure of Arab public opinion has for many years forced them to offer apparent unconditional support to the refugees' claims. It follows that the defeats of the Six-Day War have only heightened this pressure. On the other hand, the commando operations and the growing popularity of al-Fatah are dangerous to all the Arab governments. In the first place, Palestinian guerilla activities expose the "brother countries" to Israeli reprisals, for Tel Aviv holds Arab governments responsible for all operations launched from their respective territories. Jordan is, more than any other country, exposed to this risk. On February 15, 1968, for example, in the wake of a mortar barrage perpetrated by al-Fatah on the Israeli kibbutzim of the valley of Beth Hean, Israeli aircraft bombed Jordanian positions. King Hussein asked for a cease-fire through the intermediary of the United States Embassy, and Israel replied that it would not stop the bombings until he agreed to oppose the Palestinian commandos actively. Hussein accepted these conditions and proceeded to arrest a number of members of the commando groups. But a few hours later all the arrests were suspended on the instructions of Jordanian Prime Minister Bahjat Talhouni, and Hussein was forced to yield a few days later, which led to resurgence of commando operations. Whereas Jordan is thus constantly torn between the opposing pressures of the

Palestinians and the Israelis, the stronger countries like Egypt and Syria are also threatened or disturbed by the very existence of the Palestinian resistance organizations. For a long time Egypt opposed the activities of these organizations, especially in the Gaza Strip, while Syria supported them unconditionally (this support was one of the causes of the Six-Day War). Since June 1967 all the Arab countries have supported the activities of the commandos, but Syria, which has become more vulnerable since the Golan Heights were taken, has imprisoned all the Palestinian leaders there and forbidden all commando activity based on Syrian territory. Al-Fatah is still not officially recognized, and the only movement supported by the Arab League is the P.L.O., a creation of the Egyptians. For having asserted the independence of al-Fatah too publicly, Youssef Orabi, commander of al-Assifah, was assassinated in the winter of 1967. For a very long time the Syrian and Jordanian secret services have tried to destroy or infiltrate the Palestinian resistance movement. The attitude of the Arab armies has often been hostile. A member of al-Fatah declared before the Six-Day War: "We have lost more men after their return to Jordan than during the operations themselves. The Jordanian secret services, financed by the American imperialists, have received orders to kill our men" (quoted in *Les Temps Modernes*, June 1967). It should nevertheless be noted that the attitude of the regular Jordanian troops has changed. They now cover the commandos' rear with gunfire barrages, keep them informed on the movements of Israeli patrols, help them to cross the Jordan, and care for their wounded.

The assertion of the *Palestinian* character of the struggle does not fail to produce secret opposition in most Arab countries, for it condemns all of Arab policy for the last twenty years. What it calls into question in Lebanon and Jordan is the continued existence of capitalistic or feudal regimes; what it calls into question in the U.A.R. and Syria is certain types of nationalism and socialism and, in the last analysis, the whole Arab "mystique" that has been developed, most notably, by Nasser. Whereas the right wing of al-Fatah looks only to the liberation of a single Palestine, the Marxist-influenced left wing calls for "simultaneous liberation of Palestine and the Arab states."

So the only country that binds itself unequivocally to supporting the activities of al-Fatah is Algeria. Henry Boumédienne was one of the first leaders to call, in August 1967, for a popular war of liberation against Israel. "We must," he said, "put an end to the lightning warfare that Israel has adopted and impose upon the Jewish state a long war of attrition." For this purpose he actively trains Palestinian students as commandos and supplies al-Fatah with considerable financial aid through the Algerian ambassador in Beirut, Talet Chaieb. It was certainly not by chance that the P.F.L.P. rerouted the El Al airliner to Algiers; it counted on the "solidarity" of the Boumédienne government.

This latent tension among the Palestinian resistance movements and the governments in power in the Middle East tends to show that massive intervention by the Arab armies can no longer be expected to change the Middle Eastern situation (for these armies will be in no condition to fight Israel for a long time to come); only the gradual toll exacted by guerilla warfare can bring such change. The Arab countries' reservations about the effectiveness of the Palestinian guerilla movement express, in fact, only their leaders' anxiety about actions over which they have no control.

Al-Fatah plays the leading role in this emerging struggle, which may well shift the Arab-Israeli conflict to an entirely new plane and in so doing alter all the political facts in the Middle East. It is the foremost resistance movement because it is completely aware of its role, its tasks, its limitations, and its means. For the first time, comparisons with the Algerian war and the struggles of the Vietcong are not just journalism. It is no longer a question of unleashing a cataclysm on Israel, as Shukhairy dreamed, but of bringing about, through continuous guerilla activity, a radical change in Israeli thinking. There is no doubt that this fight will be prolonged, because it is necessary also to change the thinking of the Arabs and the Palestinians themselves and because Israel is still light-years away from recognizing al-Fatah as a "valid spokesman." Peace will not come to the Middle East tomorrow: All one can say about this new form of warfare is that it has changed in character and purpose.

INDEX